Hair Care & Styling
for Men

HAIR CARE & STYLING

FOR MEN

A Guide

to

Healthier

Looking

Hair

Lorin **Shields-Michel**

Maura **Scali-Sheahan**

Kenneth **Young**

PERSONAL CARE COLLECTION

DELMAR
THOMSON LEARNING

Australia   Canada   Mexico   Singapore   Spain   United Kingdom   United States

Delmar Staff:

Business Unit Director: Susan L. Simpfenderfer
Executive Editor: Marlene McHugh Pratt
Acquisitions Editor: Paul Drougas
Developmental Editor: Patricia A. Gillivan
Editorial Assistant: Rebecca McCarthy
Executive Marketing Manager: Donna J. Lewis
Channel Manager: Wendy E. Mapstone
Executive Production Manager: Wendy A. Troeger

Library of Congress Cataloging-in-Publication Data
Shields-Michel, Lorin.
    Hair care & styling for men : a guide to healthier hair / Lorin Shields-Michel, Maura Scali-Sheahan, Kenneth Young.
        p. cm. — (Personal care collection)
        Includes index.
        ISBN 0-7668-3817-X
        1. Hair—Care and hygiene. 2. Grooming for men. I. Title: Hair care and styling for men. II. Scali-Sheahan, Maura T. III. Young, Kenneth, 1952–   . IV. Title. V. Series.
    RA777.8 .S53 2001
646.7'24'081—dc21

2001047505

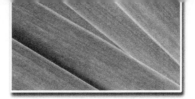

Contents

An Introduction to Hair

When he was five, Sam got his hair cut by a barber. Once every six Saturdays, his father would take him down to the corner of Fifth and Main, sit him down in a big, stiff chair, and walk outside to smoke a cigarette while the barber, a man of about seventy-five who wore Coke-bottle glasses and couldn't see to cut a straight line, would "cut" Sam's hair. Butcher, actually. The boy would cry for the entire ten minutes of his hair cut. Big, crocodile tears streamed down his cheeks as he wished for his mommy to come and save him.

The fact of the matter is that, from a very early age, most of us place a tremendous amount of importance on appearance. Nobody talks about the first time he or she took a step, but we all know how old we were when we finally got hair. It was then that our relatives started to coo over our beautiful curls and our mothers fussed about the first time those curls would need to be cut. We knew that we were cute, and we knew that our cuteness had something to do with our hair.

Perhaps that's why we place so much importance on our hairstyle as we grow older. (Notice we didn't say, "grow up.") Hair can say a lot about us. It is somehow able to make us appear distinguished, give hints about our social status and financial situation, and can even be a deciding factor in whether or not we get a date. We can say that women don't care about hair. We can even kid ourselves and say that we don't really care about whether we have male pattern hair loss. But the fact remains: hair is important to our overall sense of self.

Here's why. Hair has social importance.

Let's be honest. Looks matter. Women see hair or the lack thereof and make a judgment about you. Hair styles and types can speak volumes about you before any words are exchanged. Think about it. Soft, sexy, shoulder-length curls might mean that you're a cuddly teddy bear. Short, straight, combed-back hair with a hard-holding styling gel denotes Wall Street. Long, flyaway hair indicates that you're a free spirit, while a crew cut could mistakenly group you with an indigent affiliation or a branch of the military. A slickly bald pate with a shiny scalp can only mean that you play professional sports, are a British-born actor, or have amazing sexual confidence.

Hair is one of the first things we notice about others. Men look at a woman, see long blonde hair or shoulder-length red hair (the kind of hair that flows against a high collar) and they make a decision. It's called "having a type," and most men think they have one. These men are usually wrong, but before realizing that, they will spend years wining and dining "their type" because they are attracted to her hair. Hair is part of identity, and the sooner we come to terms with that fact, the better off we'll be.

CHANGING STYLES

Hair and its style can be directly connected to historical times, places, and most specifically, people. Recently, we've seen many men clamor for the "George Clooney" or the "Brad Pitt." Men shave their heads and polish their smooth scalps with oil-based tonics to emulate former basketball star Michael Jordan or actor Patrick Stewart. But hair and other aspects of grooming have been equated with famous figures for much longer than the past thirty years. Witness the Hitler moustache or the princely lock of the Ramses era of ancient Egypt. There's the Dali twirl, named for famous Spanish surrealistic artist Salvadore Dali, and the extreme vanity made famous by F. Scott Fitzgerald in *The Great Gatsby*.

In the late eighteenth century, the European upper class wore powdered wigs over their natural hair to distinguish themselves from the commoners. In late twentieth century films like *Dangerous Liaisons* and *A Fish Called Wanda,* the wealthy and the barristers (lawyers) all don fake hair to make themselves into something they're not. It's still common practice for British barristers to wear wigs in court. This is what vanity is all about. Thankfully, it's not necessarily what good grooming and a great hairstyle are all about. Vanity has a way of changing with the times, just as styles change.

Looking back at our most recent history, it's easy to chart the progress of style. The crew cuts of the 1940s were stylish out of necessity: buzzing off one's hair made for one less thing to worry about during World War II. The 1950s saw a young Tennessee boy with a pompadour and duck tail named Elvis Presley make young men all over the country rebel by adopting similar styles. In the 1960s, there was further rebellion. The decade started off as fairly conservative under the leadership of President John F. Kennedy with his short yet stylish shock of hair. But after his assassination in 1963 and the escalation of America's participation in the Vietnam War, the nation's young men grew their hair long, tied it back with pieces of rawhide, and kept it out of their eyes with tie-dyed headbands.

Then came Jimi Hendrix and his wild disarray of hair, jangling out from behind his peace-sign headband, setting men's styles on fire as easily as he torched his guitar. The 1970s afros were first attributed to African Americans, but it wasn't long before men of all nationalities, from Vermont to Florida to Montana to California to Hawaii, were sporting these big, frizzy, curled-out " 'fros."

Once disco managed to rid the world of style, men rebelled yet again and went into their Masters of the Universe phase, a term coined by satirical novelist Tom Wolfe in his blockbuster book on greed, *The Bonfire of the Vanities.* It was 1984. Haircuts were short again, slicked back with high-powered gel and held in place with a Wall Street attitude. The 1980s were a time of style conscience and extreme self-consciousness tied up in straight hair, shaved faces, and pinstripes.

It's been pretty much the same since then, with some minor variations. Men, women, and children all have fairly responsible and conservative hairstyles. We all trot off to see our hairstylist or barber every four to six weeks for a trim, maybe a shave, so that we look good as we go off to work, attend the kid's soccer game, go out to dinner, or have a weekend away from the rat-race of life.

But what does it all mean? Where did style originate? Why do we all strive to achieve what society determines is "perfect"? Perhaps it all has something to do with changing times, changing styles, and the enduring desire to be attractive to the opposite sex. Admit it: If she thinks a particular hairstyle is sexy, you'll wear it.

HOW HAIR MIRRORS THE TIMES

Hair cuts and styles mirror the trends of society. Whether it be counter-culture, conservative, or an individual statement against the establishment, personal style and how it's achieved are here to stay.

We've seen how hairstyles have changed through the centuries and through the most recent decades. Our ability to change allows us to stay modern.

In this book, we'll look at several issues that affect how we deal with our hair, from types of hair and how to treat it most effectively, to hair's actual chemical structure, to specific styles and products that create the exact look you're seeking. We'll deal with hair loss, sometimes referred to as male-pattern baldness, or, in this book, as being follicle-ly challenged. We'll discuss how best to keep what you've got and recover what you've lost. We'll also discuss optical illusions, or the now-you've-got-gray-hair, now-you-don't color options that are available, from permanent hair color changes to temporary washes that will change your look for just a day or two.

When it comes to hair and its ever-changing styles, you need look no further than the following pages to discover that what's hair today can also be hair tomorrow.

Types of Hair

Hair type contributes to each person's individuality, his mark. Hair type can be categorized four ways: straight, wavy, curly, and kinky. Straight hair is the roundest of the four categories and kinky is the flattest. Curly hair tends to grow straight up and out from the scalp, giving the impression of more hair, while straighter hair types lie closer to the head.

HAIR GRAIN

Hair grain is very much like wood grain. When you look at a piece of oak, pine, walnut, or other type of wood, you can see the direction it flows based on how the lines present themselves. Sanding and dusting is always done "with the grain" in order to eliminate scratches. The direction that hair grows is considered its grain. Hair grain dictates the way hair is cut and ultimately the way it's styled.

Bob Ohnstad, in his book *Scissors and Comb Haircutting* (You Can Publishing, 1997), describes grain in this way: "Run your hand through the hair on [a dog's] back from tail to head: the hair stands on end for a moment, then lies down again, returning to its natural lying position." That defines the dog's hair-grain pattern.

People are dogs, at least for the sake of this illustration, because our hair grain can be defined the same way. It's important to know that hair does not grow straight up. Even when cut into a crew-cut style, hair grows back at an angle.

Most heads of hair grow in one of two patterns.

1. *The 40% rule.* This pattern occurs when the side hair grows toward the ground. It's usually found in people with straight hair, and accounts for approximately 40% of the people in the world.

2. *The 60% rule.* Obviously, if 40% of the world's hair population grows toward the ground, then it's only logical that the rest of the world has wavy, curly, or kinky hair that grows in all kinds of directions. The easiest way to spot a 60%er is to look at how the hair grows on the back of the neck. If it's growing in curves, instead of straight down, you're looking at one.

CROWNED WITH A COWLICK

There are exceptions to every rule, and in the realm of hair care and styling they're called cowlicks. Cowlicks are often characterized as wildly irregular tufts of hair, a group of strands that grow in a direction completely contrary to the rest of the hair. Cowlicks are almost always maligned and cursed. We wage war on them every minute of every day, from the moment we get up to the time we go to bed, because we believe—and rightly so—that cowlicks are the enemy.

Would it give you any comfort to know that everyone has a cowlick? They grow in the upper back part of the head—the crown—and some people are lucky enough to actually have two. The ones that truly wreak havoc on a good hairstyle are those that show themselves at the front of the hairline. However cranky cowlicks may be, they are important for one reason: they establish the center of the hair-grain pattern.

Hair that grows from a cowlick in the crown grows out and away from the head, giving hair its "Dennis-the-Menace" look. The crown cowlick grows down toward the bottom of the neck at the same time that it's growing up toward the front of the top of the head. A left-sided cowlick grows up and out from the center of the crown, with most hair growing off to the right. It's the exact opposite of a right-sided cowlick, with hair growing to the left. Center cowlicks can grow any number of ways, with the cowlick hair growing up and out, spinning off either to the left, the right, or straight ahead.

So what gives, since it's obviously not your hair? And can cowlicks be tamed? Even the wildest tigers can be tamed, so it's a safe bet to say that yes, cowlicks can, in fact, be tamed. They can also be hidden. Long straight hair is heavy and bends hair toward the scalp at the root. Because of this phenomenon, the cowlick is also pulled down and harder to see. Cutting hair relieves the weight and allows the cowlick to "come up for air."

In curlier hair types, a cowlick can actually get confused because the hair grows out of the scalp in odd spring-shapes. Even in shorter hairstyles it's hard to find a cowlick in a mass of curls or waves, but cut the hair very short, and once again the crown cowlick will reveal itself.

Front line cowlicks can be exaggerated by combing and styling hair against its natural grain. If your hair naturally grows to the left, and you insist on combing it to the right, previously camouflaged cowlicks will appear. The solution, of course, is to comb hair in the direction it wants to go.

Cowlicks can also appear at the nape, or base, of the neck as well as lower down from the crown. Essentially, cowlicks can appear anywhere and almost everywhere, but they can be handled easily as long as you know that you have one (or two) and style accordingly. Your hairstylist or barber is well versed in judging hair grain and spotting cowlicks, so when you get a haircut, follow his or her recommendation. Your stylist probably has a better vantage point when it comes to working with your cowlick, taming it, and helping you learn to live with it. Remember: everyone does have one, so you're not alone.

DOES NATURAL COLOR HAVE ANYTHING TO DO WITH TEXTURE?

Texture relates to the thickness or lack thereof in each individual hair. A hair's diameter can be as thick as 1/100 of an inch, or as thin as 1/500 of an inch, with the former being considered thick, the latter being fine, and somewhere in the middle categorized as medium. Finer hair also tends to be softer to the touch while thicker hair feels coarse. Medium hair thickness falls somewhere in between soft and coarse in its texture.

Chemical hair color will change the feel of hair because chemicals change the cuticle of the hair. As most of us know, chemicals can be damaging even if they help us achieve what we need or want. Permanent hair color will alter hair's natural makeup, thus altering its texture. We'll talk more about that in Chapter 7.

It is important to realize that hair stylists and barbers often talk about hair as being thick or thin, referring to the amount of hairs that grow per square inch of scalp. Obviously, the more hairs, the thicker the feel.

Age can also influence the texture of hair. Most people are born with little or no hair. What is there is usually extraordinarily fine, hence the term "baby-fine." As we grow toward puberty, hair expands in texture. In early adulthood, prior to hair changing to gray, our hair is at its optimum texture: fine, medium, or thick. As we age and our hair loses its pigmentation, turning white, silver, or gray, it often acquires a new texture. What was fine can become medium, medium can feel thick, and thick can get downright coarse, or "wiry."

AFRICAN AMERICAN

African American hair tends to range from curly to very kinky. It quite often has a coarse texture. If you're African American, you probably have more hairs per square inch on your head than others. However, you come in second when it comes to losing your hair. More on that in Chapter 6.

Most haircuts and styles are adaptable to this type of hair, though a cut that's the same length all around, whether long or short, is the easiest and most popular. Coarse hair is also easier to handle with a large, heavy-duty comb, sometimes called a *pick*.

Hair's Structure

Hair, like any other part of the body, is made up of parts whose chemistry is amazing but also quite confusing. The fact that hair even has a chemistry, considering it is by scientific accounts not truly alive, is quite startling in itself. But here it is: Hair is made up of keratin, a protein that is also prevalent in the nails as well as the skin. Hair's chemical composition is approximately 50 percent carbon, 20 percent oxygen, 20 percent nitrogen, 5 percent sulfur, and 5 percent hydrogen.

Hair is made up of four separate and distinct parts that can chart its age, similar to how we chart the age of a tree by looking at its rings. The four parts are as follows.

1. End (the oldest part of the hair)
2. Hairshaft (the part of hair that is visible, from scalp to end)
3. Root (the part of hair that is beneath the skin or scalp)
4. Bulb (the youngest, newest part of the hair, often categorized by the small bump at the bottom of the hair. This bump can actually be seen and felt when the hair is pulled or falls out.)

Hair also has three distinct layers, found by examining the hairshaft.

1. The cuticle, the outermost layer of the hairshaft, consists of hard, flattened, spiky scales that overlap each other. There are usually five to seven layers found in one scale, allowing for a very strong yet flexible

arrangement. Visualize roof tiles. The cuticle functions to protect hair. If hair is healthy, the scales lie flat and show off their shine. If the cuticle is damaged, the scales will curl, making the hair appear dull. Some types of damage can occur from chemicals such as hair color, perms, and relaxers. If the cuticle is damaged, then the interior of the hair is damaged, leading to common problems like split ends and fly-aways. That interior layer is known as the *cortex*.

2. The cortex makes up between 75 percent and 90 percent of each hair. Its overall health determines the hair's strength, elasticity, pliability, direction of growth, thickness, and texture. The cortex contains melanin, the pigment that gives color to hair. The cortex is made up of millions of parallel fibers of keratin that form what is commonly known in the hair-care industry as *polypeptide chains*. These chains function like other chains, linking together for strength. Made up of chemical components like hydrogen, sulfur, or peptides, these chains can be changed easily with physical components like water, gels, mousses, and other styling aids. They can also be altered chemically.

3. The medulla is the innermost layer of hair. Not much is known about this layer although it is generally referred to as a sponge-like substance that works to expel unwanted invaders of each strand. The medulla may not exist in hair with smaller diameters.

This chapter, discussing hair's structure, would not be complete without a discussion about the follicle. Many people have heard about the follicle. There are even jokes about being follicle-ly challenged, a topic covered in Chapter 6. However, most people aren't entirely sure what constitutes a follicle. It is defined as a sheath that surrounds the lower, subcutaneous part of the hair. More accurately, it's a part of the skin that surrounds the hair's root and bulb. It also produces the keratin cells that make up a growing hair, is about a quarter-inch deep, and, like all other components of the hair, has parts.

1. The papilla, or the site of hair's cell production, is the living part of the follicle. It is what causes pain when hair is pulled.

2. The blood vessel, which supplies nourishment and helps the papilla to create new cells.

3. The nerve supply, which regulates the follicle, and sends out brain signals for pain when the papilla is pulled. This nerve system also turns itself off once the hair reaches a specific age.

4. The sebaceous glands produce hair's natural oils, often called *sebum.* This sebum travels from the gland all the way to the ends of the hair. The glands don't produce much sebum prior to puberty and slow down noticeably after age fifty.

Hair grows at varying rates. This variation is one of the factors that make each individual different from all others. Like a fingerprint, hair can be used to make a person distinct. DNA can be found inside each hair. So how many hairs grow, how fast do they grow, and does growth rate differ depending on hair color? The answers are: a bunch, it depends, and yes.

Hair has approximately 120 square inches of growing surface on the adult scalp, producing approximately 1,000 hairs per square inch. An interesting fact that many people aren't aware of is that each person is born with a finite amount of hair-producing follicles. We do not grow new follicles as we age. Some even stop producing hair.

The rate of hair growth is directly related to diameter and hair color. Fine, light-colored hair grows approximately 3/8 inch per month. Other hair types usually grow as much as 3/4 inch per month, though the average is usually about 1/2 inch. Dark hair generally grows faster than light hair. Coarse hair grows faster than fine hair. Unfortunately, gray hair generally grows faster than the pigmented hair it replaces, so we not only have to contend with a new type of hair as we age, but need to have that hair trimmed more often.

Hair also has a lifespan of just two to four years per strand. At the end of its life, it separates painlessly from the follicle. You'll usually find it in your sink, on the floor, or circling your shower drain.

Hair color truly does make a difference in terms of how much hair we have. If you're blonde, you're the winner, with an average of 120,000 hairs on your head. Dark-haired folks have about 110,000 hairs, while redheads seem to have the least amount of hair, checking in at just 95,000. Growth rates remain the same for those in the 100,000 club. It's only the very young or the getting-older who contend with different growth rates: children two and younger have slower rates than the distinguished and debonair gray-hairs.

WHY WE HAVE HAIR

Hair doesn't just give you style or put you under undo pressure to conform to style. It also serves a very real function: protection. It protects us from extreme cold as well as unbearable heat. In the winter, during those cold, snowy months, heat escapes through the top of the head. In fact, bald men lose body heat much faster than those with a full head of hair. In the warm summer months, hair insulates against extreme heat. Again, bald men are more apt to fall victim to heat stroke than men with full heads of hair.

Hair also offers some protection against blows to the head that might harm the fragile brain. Perhaps that's why its treatment has garnered so much attention over the years.

CHAPTER 4

Treating Hair

E arly hair care involved the use of soured milk, rotting fruits, and animal fat. Luckily, we've progressed to the point of protein enhancers, hydrating cleansers, and noncombative fragrances that combine to make today's hair care a generally pleasing experience from shower to shower.

Hair care can easily be divided into three components: shampoos, conditioners, and styling tools, all of which affect the outcome of your hairstyle.

Before we get into the specifics, we should talk a little about pH. Ultimately, hair is directly affected by the acidity or alkalinity present. Acidity, or the state of being excessively acid, is bad for hair. Acidity has an adverse effect on hair's look and feel, causing it to shrink and feel almost hard to the touch. Alkalinity, from the word *alkali,* actually swells hair too much, often giving a fly-away feel. Water represents the perfect pH of 7, whereas hair generally falls into the 4.5 to 5.5 range. In order to raise hair to the perfect pH of 7, it is preferable to use pH-balanced shampoos. High alkaline shampoos give the impression of scrubbing the hair clean, leaving it almost squeaky, but if used too often, these shampoos (with pH levels of 7 to 10) will lead to split ends and hair breakage.

Let's talk about how best to treat hair, beginning with shampoo.

SHAMPOOS

The primary purpose of shampooing is to clean the scalp and hair. To be effective, a shampoo must remove all dirt, oil, perspiration, and skin debris without adversely affecting the scalp or the hair.

The hair collects dust particles, natural oils from the sebaceous glands, perspiration, and dead skin cells that accumulate on the scalp. This accumulation creates a breeding place for disease-producing bacteria that, in turn, can lead to scalp disorders. The hair and scalp should be thoroughly shampooed as frequently as is necessary to keep them clean, healthy, and free from bacteria.

An effective shampoo has four characteristics.

1. It cleanses the hair of oils, debris, and dirt.

2. It works efficiently in hard as well as soft water.

3. It does not irritate the eyes or skin.

4. It leaves hair and scalp in their most natural condition.

How does shampoo really work? It all has to do with molecules.

Shampoo molecules are large and specially treated. They are composed of a head and a tail, each with its own special function. The tail attracts dirt, grease, debris, and oil, but repels water. The head of the shampoo molecule attracts water, but repels dirt. By working together, both parts of the molecule effectively cleanse the hair.

Cleansing hair is not just dependent on shampoo. It's also dependent on the type of water that you use when washing your hair, categorized either as hard or soft. Hard water contains certain minerals. As a result, shampoo doesn't lather very well. But don't despair. Hard water can usually be softened by chemical processes, making it suitable for shampooing. Soft water is water that has been chemically softened. It contains very small amounts of minerals, causing it to help shampoo to lather more easily. Consequently, it's preferred for shampooing.

What is it about shampoos that make them good for your hair? To determine which shampoo will leave hair in the best condition, you need to have an understanding of shampoo ingredients.

Shampoo Ingredients

Water is the primary ingredient in all shampoos. Usually it isn't just plain tap water, but purified or de-ionized water. The second ingredient is a cleansing or surface active agent, also known as a *surfactant*. The list of ingredients goes on from there, often including botanicals, extracts, vitamins, sunscreens, and moisturizers.

Types of Shampoos

Shampoos fall into several categories. There are many that are geared toward specific hair types, as well as those for specific scalp conditions. Normally, the front of a shampoo bottle will tell you exactly what type of hair it's for, with such descriptions as "normal," "normal to dry," and "normal to oily." These descriptions usually refer to the scalp condition because oils or lack of oils on the scalp also influence the hair's condition.

- *Plain shampoos* are usually clear. They're great for hair that is in good condition, and shouldn't be used on chemically treated hair (meaning colored, permed, or relaxed) because they can dry hair as well as strip color.

- *Medicated shampoos* contain a medicinal agent like sulphur, tar, cresol, phenol, or other antiseptic.

- *Therapeutic medicated shampoos* contain special chemicals or drugs that reduce excessive conditions like dandruff.

- *Acid-balanced shampoos* are mild, moisturizing shampoos that are great for normal and chemically treated hair. These types of shampoos won't strip hair of color.

- *Moisturizing or conditioning shampoos* are mild, creamy shampoos that contain humectants and hydrators that lock moisture into hair.

- *Clarifying shampoos* are stronger shampoos that remove excess dirt, oils, pollutants, and excessive styling product residue from hair. These are great cleansers after a strenuous workout.

- *Organic shampoos* contain natural ingredients like botanicals and extracts, aloe vera, chamomile, and jojoba. They're almost always pH balanced so they don't over- or under-cleanse.

- *Cleansing or chelating shampoos* remove iron deposited by well water.

CONDITIONERS AND WHY YOU NEED THEM

Home conditioners didn't become popular until the 1970s. It was during this time that both men and women started to experiment with hair color and perms, damaging their hair. Of course, women have been damaging their hair for centuries in the never-ending quest for beauty. Now, suddenly, men were in the picture. The rebellious nature of the ravaged sixties contributed to a new attitude, and, let's face it, bad hair. Frizzed out 'fros and chemical colors, constant blow drying, sun exposure, and other types of damage made hair look and feel like straw.

Enter conditioners. Designed to deposit protein or moisturizers into damaged areas of abused hair, conditioners give the hair body and shine while also making it easier to comb.

Conditioners are often used to prepare hair before a chemical service. They help to restore natural oils and proteins as well as to moisturize the hair. If you have dry, brittle hair, you'll also benefit from regular conditioning treatments.

Available in both cream and liquid forms, conditioners may contain lanoline, moisturizers, fatty acids, vegetable oils, proteins, herbs, organic substances, and combinations of all of these. For optimum results, it's important to follow instructions on the back panel of your chosen conditioner. Most are applied to damp hair and rinsed out after a given amount of time. Leave-in conditioners work to treat hair while also adding a bit of style.

Type of Conditioners

Five general groups of hair conditioners are available: instant, leave-in, protein, neutralizing, and moisturizing. What's best for your hair depends on the texture and condition of your hair, as well as what you want your end result to be.

- *Instant*—These conditioners are applied to hair, left on for one to five minutes depending on directions, and then rinsed out. They usually have an acid pH, which helps to close the cuticle scales. They don't penetrate into the hair shaft, but they do add oils, moisture, and a bit of protein to slightly damaged hair.

- *Conditioner/styling lotions*—Also known as *leave-in conditioners,* these lotions are protein or resin-based. Worked into hair when the hair is damp, they help to facilitate styling by keeping hair soft and manageable. These conditioners are designed to temporarily increase the hair's diameter by using a coating action that actually gives body. They're available in several strengths to accommodate various textures, conditions, and hair qualities.

- *Protein*—These conditioners utilize hydrolyzed protein (very small fragments), moisturizers, and oils. The hydrolyzed protein passes through the cuticle to penetrate the cortex where the keratin has been lost. These conditioners improve texture, equalize porosity, and help increase elasticity in hair. When using a protein conditioner, hair should be thoroughly rinsed before styling.

- *Neutralizing*—Also known as *pH balancers,* these conditioners neutralize alkalinity created by strong alkaline products. They have an acid pH and are designed to prevent damage to hair while also helping to alleviate scalp irritation. Neutralizing conditioners are usually left on the hair from one to five minutes before rinsing.

- *Moisturizing*—These conditioners draw moisture into the hair with humectants. Humectants are chemical compounds that absorb and hold moisture, sealing it inside damp hair by coating the cuticle. Natural moisturizing ingredients may include oils, essential fatty acids, sodium PCA, and some botanicals.

There are also other types of vegetable, protein, and synthetic polymer conditioners available. These are highly specialized conditioners.

- *Synthetic polymer conditioner*—A polymer is a compound consisting of many repeated units that form a chain. When hair is badly damaged and seemingly can't be restored, synthetic polymers are brought in to prevent breakage and to help correct excessive porosity.

- *Chelators*—Also known as *clarifiers,* these types of treatments are usually used before coloring or perming. Chelators neutralize, or remove, metallic elements in hair that might interfere with the chemicals being applied. A chelator can be either a separate conditioner or an ingredient in a pretreatment product. This isn't anything you necessarily need to worry about. Your stylist will use one if it's needed.

HOME REMEDIES

When you've run out of shampoo, desperately need a conditioner, and you just can't get to the store, experiment with what's in the kitchen.

Eggs aren't just great breakfast food. They also make a nifty shampoo. Wash the egg, crack it into a bowl, and beat thoroughly. Wet your hair and apply half of the egg, working it into a semi-lather. Rinse in lukewarm water. (This is important: Do not, under any circumstance, rinse with hot water. You'll get the equivalent of scrambled eggs in your hair.) Repeat the process with the second half of the egg.

For a nice finish, apply a lemon rinse. Lemon rinses are made by squeezing half a lemon into two cups of water. Pour this mixture over the hair.

You can use a vinegar rinse by adding three to four tablespoons of vinegar to two cups of water. After using either of these rinses, rinse hair again with warm water. Don't worry about smelling like lemons or vinegar. Any residual odor disappears once hair is dry.

Mayonnaise may be great on a turkey sandwich, but it's even better in hair. Measure out a couple of tablespoons of mayo, work it through hair, leave it on for two hours, and then rinse. Rinse very well. Your hair will be softer and more manageable than ever.

Olive oil also makes a great treatment. Apply about an ounce of olive oil to freshly shampooed hair, working it through evenly. Then wrap your head in a steaming hot towel and place a plastic bag over the towel, sealing in the heat. Leave it on for about ten minutes and then shampoo as usual. Keep in mind that you might need to shampoo two or three times, or use two or three eggs, to remove the oil.

STYLING TOOLS

After you've shampooed and conditioned, you're ready to style. Hundreds of gels, mousses, creams, pomades, and hair sprays are available. You name it. If you can put it in your hair after you've showered, you can style with it.

Ever since retail products like Dippity-Do in the 1960s and 1970s were introduced, we've been hooked on the idea of styling. Sculpted styling actually started in the 1950s, when the pompadour was made popular by Elvis Presley and James Dean. These cult icons sported slickly styled hair that hugged the head on the side and reached toward a point—the ducktail—in the back. On the top, they fashioned an exaggerated poof of hair, carefully combed and held in place by petroleum jelly.

That's right. Petroleum jelly was one of the first styling products used by men to keep their hair in place all day and into the night. Of course, getting it out was a huge undertaking.

Products like butch wax, a substance that resembled lard, were among the earliest forms of pomade, giving hair a greasy, unkempt, sexy look. Then came Brylcream, a lighter-weight, greasy gel-paste that was the precursor to today's gel. Vitalis was a liquid gel that poured easily into the hands and was worked through hair, allowing you to "shape" the hair. When dry, Vitalis was hard, almost helmet-like. Hair didn't move even in high winds.

Luckily we don't have that problem today. There are hundreds of different styling tools from which to choose. The retail shelves of salons and barber shops today are almost as crowded as those in the grocery stores and drug stores. The number and variety of products can be a bit confusing. The trick is to ask. Ask your hairstylist. Ask your wife, your sister, your girlfriend, your partner. Ask a friend what he uses to get his hair to "do that," and you'll have an idea of how to proceed.

Here's an abridged version of styling products and what they can do for your hair.

1. *Gels*—Usually resin-based and clear in color, gels provide anywhere from medium to extreme hold. Simply pour or squeeze, depending on packaging, into your hands, rub them together, and then run your hands through your hair for even distribution. Follow the manufacturer's directions.

2. *Pomades*—These are creamy, wax-types of styling tools normally found in a pot or jar. Scoop the pomade out and apply to hair for a flexible hold and movable body.

3. *Mousses*—These foams are usually used with a blowdryer to increase body and volume. They don't provide much hold or control, but they do serve a function. They make hair appear bigger, and bigger is sometimes better.

4. *Creams*—These are lightweight lotions that provide benefits similar to those of a gel.

5. *Hair sprays*—Sometimes a little blast of hold is all you need. Hair sprays are usually aerosols or liquids in pumps.

With any styling tool, you should follow manufacturer's directions. If you don't know what you should use, experiment. Your wife or girlfriend probably has any number of styling tools under the sink. She'll be glad to show you how to use them. After awhile, you'll develop your own style and your own preference.

COMBS AND BRUSHES

Combs are available in a variety of styles and sizes. The correct comb to use depends on individual preference. Combs can be made of hard rubber, bone, or plastic. Because of the cost, combs made of bone are not very popular. The teeth of the comb may be fine (close together) or coarse (far apart). It's important that the teeth have rounded ends to avoid scratching or irritating the scalp.

A number of different types of brushes are widely available. The choice of bristle texture, spacing, and material will depend on the hairstyle desired. Using a brush properly can produce waving, add fullness and smoothness, and stimulate the scalp.

Hair brushes are made out of plastic, wood, or metal, and contain either natural or artificial bristles. Some brush styles combine plastic or hard rubber handles with a cushioned rubber base into which either nylon or metal bristles are set.

There's actually a way to pick the right brush to make your head look better. It involves a highly scientific method: you have to know your hair type and style. Here's how it works.

Thick, coarse hair needs a natural-bristle brush. Something made out of wild boar seems appropriate for a wild mane, and is actually easier to pull through thick hair. It can also help distribute natural oils, making your hair look more tame.

A short buzz begs for a plastic-tip brush. The hard bristles will move hair easily into place and help get rid of dandruff by stimulating your scalp's blood flow.

Thin, straight hair is best with a brush called the "classic styler." Nylon bristles seem to have the ability to make thin hair look taller because they make the hair stand a bit taller.

A vent brush is perfect for wavy hair. This type of brush literally has the nylon bristles coming out from slats in the brush head. The bristles have rounded tips, allowing you to shape your hair into place without ignoring its natural texture.

For curly hair, stick with a wide-tooth comb. It's less likely to get stuck in the curls because of the distance between the teeth.

And if all else fails, you can always shave your head. More on that in Chapter 9.

SHEARS

You should have a pair of haircutting shears, not because you're expected to cut your own hair, but because often one side grows faster than the other and needs a little trim. You may also have that wayward lock that sticks out and that no amount of gel or spray will make stay in place. Break out the shears and cut. Carefully.

Styling Hair

A good hair cut is worth its lack of weight in gold. A good hair cut makes your hair look and feel healthier than it was before. A good hair cut can be low maintenance, so much so that you can wash and go without having to constantly worry about your hair. A good hair cut actually can make you feel better about yourself. The phrase "good hair day" had to come from somewhere and mean something. When you get rid of the hairs around your ears or at the base of your neck, it feels good, just as it feels good to run your hands through freshly cut hair. When you feel good, you look good and when you look good, you feel good.

FACIAL TYPES

How do you know what cut is best for you? Sometimes the key is simply a matter of studying and knowing your facial type. Facial type is determined by the position and prominence of the facial bones. There are seven facial types: oval, round, triangular, square, pear-shaped, oblong, and diamond. While no amount of exercise will change the basic facial shape, hairstyles can complement facial shape in much the same way certain clothes flatter the body.

Here are some general rules.

■ *Oval facial type*—The oval-shaped face is generally recognized as the ideal shape. Any hairstyle is suitable. Try changing the part. Experiment—keeping in mind elements such as lifestyle, comfort, and ease of maintenance. (Figure 5-1)

FIGURE 5-1 Oval face

FIGURE 5-2 Round face

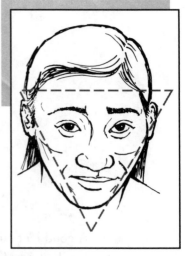

FIGURE 5-3 Triangular face

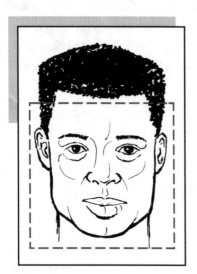

FIGURE 5-4 Square face

- *Round facial type*—The aim here is to slim the face. Hair that's too short will emphasize fullness. An off-center part and some waves at eye level will help lessen the full appearance. Beards should be styled to make the face appear oval. (Figure 5-2)

- *Triangular facial type*—The potential problems with this facial shape are over-wide cheekbones and a very narrow chin. Keep the hair close to the crown and temples and longer and fuller in back. A full beard helps to fill out a narrow jaw. (Figure 5-3)

- *Square facial type*—To minimize the angular features at the forehead, use wavy bangs that blend into the temples. This softens the square forehead and draws attention to a strong jaw. If a beard is worn, it should be styled to slenderize the face. (Figure 5-4)

- *Pear-shaped facial type*—This shape is narrow at the top and wide on the bottom. Volume and fullness at the crown and temples are necessary to provide balance. Short, full styles are best, ending just above the jawline. A good perm could be another way to achieve width at the

FIGURE 5-5 Pear-shaped face   **FIGURE 5-6** Oblong face   **FIGURE 5-7** Diamond face

top. If a beard is worn, it should be styled to slenderize the lower jaw. (Figure 5-5)

- *Oblong facial type*—The long face needs to be shortened, the angularity hidden, the hairline never exposed. A layered cut is best. A mustache helps to shorten a long face. (Figure 5-6)

- *Diamond facial type*—The hair is styled to fill out the face at the temples and chin and kept close to the head at the widest points. Deep, full bangs give a broad appearance to the forehead and a one-length cut in the back adds width. A full, square, or rounded beard would also be appropriate. (Figure 5-7)

PROFILES

When creating a hairstyle, the profile can be a good indicator as to the correct shape of hairstyle to choose.

- *Straight*—All hairstyles usually are becoming to the straight profile. (Figure 5-8)

- *Concave*—Requires close hair arrangement over the forehead to minimize the bulge of the forehead. (Figure 5-9)

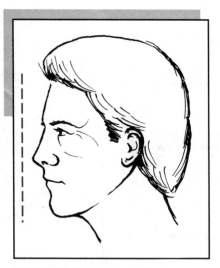

FIGURE 5-8 Straight profile

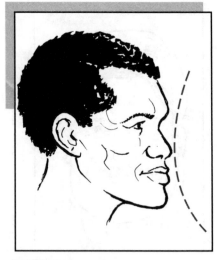

FIGURE 5-9 Concave profile (prominent forehead and chin)

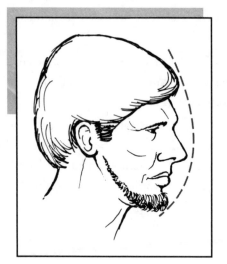

FIGURE 5-10 Convex profile (receding forehead, prominent nose, and receding chin)

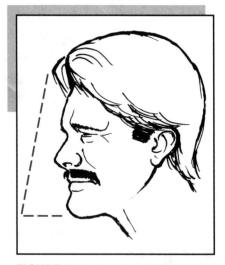

FIGURE 5-11 Angular profile

■ *Convex*—To conceal a short, receding forehead, arrange the top front hair over the forehead. A beard minimizes a receding chin. (Figure 5-10)

■ *Angular*—Hair that is drawn forward to conceal a receding forehead. A short beard and mustache help to minimize a protruding chin. (Figure 5-11)

NOSE SHAPES

Nose shapes are closely related to profile. When studying your face, consider the nose both in profile and in full face.

- *Prominent nose*—A hooked nose, a large nose, or a pointed nose all come under this classification. To minimize the prominence of the nose, bring the hair forward at the forehead and back at the sides. (Figure 5-12)

- *Turned-up nose*—Comb the hair down over the forehead and back at the sides. (Figure 5-13)

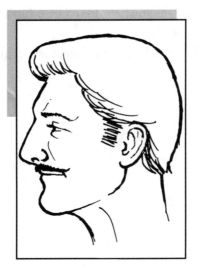

FIGURE 5-12 Prominent nose

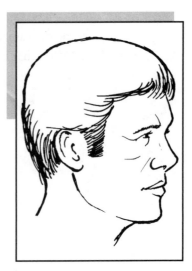

FIGURE 5-13 Turned-up nose

NECK

The length of the neck should also be a factor in determining the overall shape of the hairstyle. The length, height, fullness, and partings of the hair should be considered when deciding which style would best complement your neck size. Leave the hair full or longer at the neck to minimize the appearance of a long neck. Leave the neck exposed to create an appearance of length.

CUTS THAT MAKE THE CUT

From long hair to a short buzz, all hair needs to be cut. Choosing the perfect cut for you begins with knowing and accepting your comfort level. If you're looking for something in particular, sometimes it's helpful to look in magazines or ask a loved one what she likes. But be careful: the latest Hollywood heartthrob may have completely different hair than yours. Ultimately, when choosing a style, you have to know that you can live with it. Talk to your hairstylist or barber. Communication is key in getting a cut that you like, that's easy to care for, and that will complement your personality, not to mention your face.

Know your hair type and texture. Go for something easy to care for and relatively low maintenance. You don't want to be spending an hour on your hair every morning. Get a haircut that fits you. If you're tall, longer hair will probably suit you. If you're short, your hair should be short. Short foreheads mean shorter tops and bangs. Long sideburns are great for long faces, but tend to look completely wrong on a smaller, shorter face.

With that in mind, let's check out some cuts for specific types of hair.

Style 1

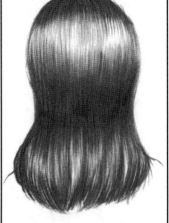

Recommended hair type: Long, one length in back with tendency to curl on the ends the longer the hair is. Also tends to be straighter when cut short.

Styling Technique

Using a diffuser with the blow dryer, dry back section in a natural fall position. Use gel to sculpture sides back; follow with the nozzle attachment and dryer. Top section may be dried to the side or back, depending on the growth pattern and your preference.

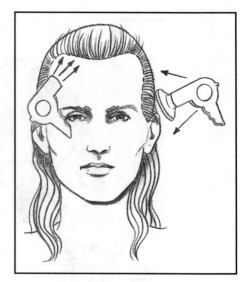

A "scrunching" technique may be used for a more texturized look, especially in the layered version. Using a diffuser attachment, blow dry back section allowing natural wave or curl to form. "Scrunch" if necessary. Top section should be dried off the face, using the fingers to lift and direct the hair back, and to create additional texture and movement. Mist with freezing spray to lock in the style.

Style 2

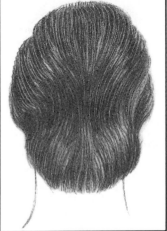

Recommended hair type: Medium to thick density; fine or medium texture; straight or slight wave formation.

Styling Technique

Apply gel or sculpting lotion, comb into place, and let dry naturally; or blow dry back section slightly, followed by brush and blow drying. Arrange straight hair or straighten wave formation with brush and blow dryer. Brush top section back to determine natural part and let fall accordingly. Brush top section back and blend with hair over the back of the ears. Use a firm holding spray for control.

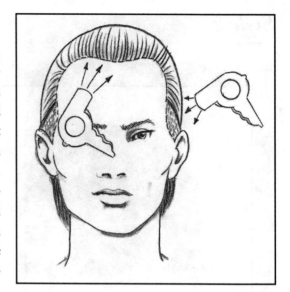

Style 3

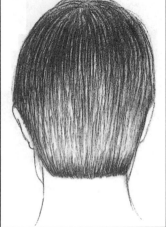

Recommended hair type: Fine to medium texture; any density except ultra-thin.

Styling Technique

Blow dry the back and sides down and the top slightly forward. Follow with directional nozzle attachment on dryer and brush hair to the side for a side part or back on the sides for a feathered look. Finish with a light holding spray.

Style 4

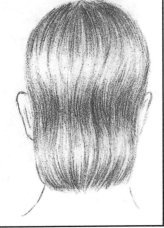

Recommended hair type: Fine, thinning hair with or without wave pattern; even distribution of hair loss in top section or up to 50 percent loss in crown area only. Also appropriate for thicker hair density types.

Styling Technique

Wavy hair type: Evenly distribute mousse through the top section for added fullness. Use a light application of gel on back section. Blow dry hair using a diffuser to allow for natural wave formation in back section. Finger comb top and side sections back for a full, textured look. Finish with a light holding spray, if needed.

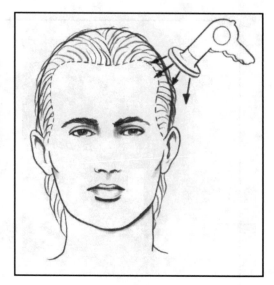

Straighter hair type: Evenly distribute mousse through top section. Using blow dryer, blow dry the back and side sections. Finger comb top section back, followed by blow dryer, to create an off the face direction and style. Finish with light holding spray.

Style 5

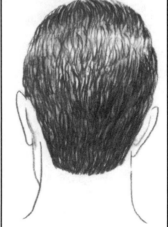

Recommended hair type: Thick, coarse, or wiry hair; even distribution; straight, wavy, or curly.

Styling Technique

Very thick hair may be combed into place and allowed to dry naturally. If a blow dryer is used, use it to follow the styling brush while hair is brushed into place. Brush the back down; brush the front and sides back. Finish with holding spray, if necessary.

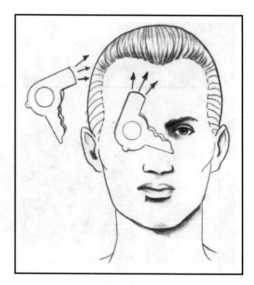

Style 6

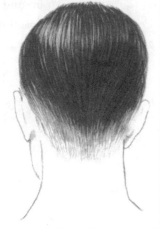

Recommended hair type: Straight to slightly wavy; medium to thick density.

Styling Techniques

For a close to the head "wet look," use sculpting lotion or gel dispersed through the hair. Comb hair down in the back, back on the sides, and from a side part on top into the natural lines of the cut. Let dry naturally.

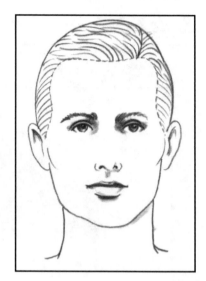

Use a gel to provide the hair with real holding power and direction to create a sculpted, casual look. Apply gel and comb the back and sides into place. Using the blow dryer and fingers, finger comb the hair on top, blending into the side hair. Using a "freezing" spray, fingers, and dryer, lift and direct front section up and slightly forward to create a low-elevation spiked look over the forehead.

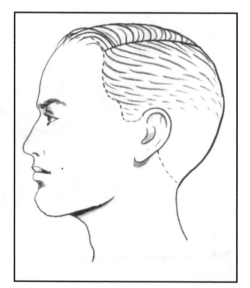

Style 7

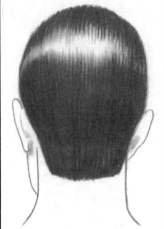

Recommended hair type: Coarse, thick, straight hair.

Styling Technique

This type of hair should be conditioned regularly with a deep moisturizing conditioner to maintain optimum pliability. Blow dry hair following the growth pattern and cut; do not free-form blow dry as extra volume is seldom needed. Instead, follow your brush with the blow dryer and nozzle attachment to concentrate air flow in a specific area. Gel or a light oil-based hair tonic will provide more styling control. For a casual look, leave hair in natural position over the forehead. For a more tailored effect, use a firm sculpting gel and spray to direct hair off the face to the side.

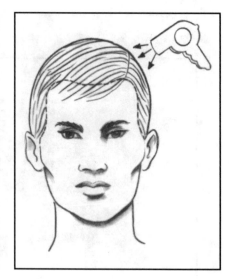

Style 8

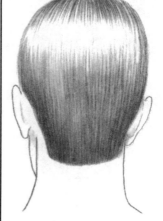

Recommended hair type: Thinning, evenly distributed; fine, or medium texture.

Styling Technique

Blow dry the back and sides to add volume. Follow with a brush for control. Part the hair on the side and blend the top section with the sides. Allow the top to air dry. Finish with light holding spray for control.

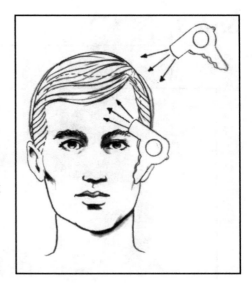

Style 9

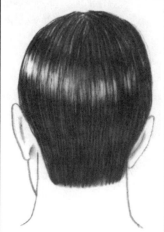

Recommended hair type: Thinning and receding hair; fine to coarse textures.

Styling Technique

Use mousse or leave-in blow-drying spray for volume; blow dry hair on the sides and back. Dry top section from left side and blend with temporal areas on right side. Finish with a light holding spray for control.

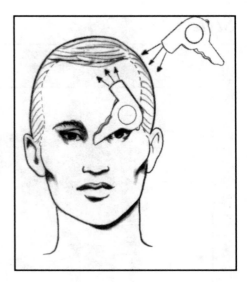

Style 10

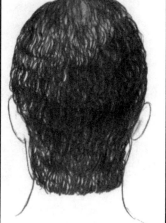

Recommended hair type: Thinning, receding, curly to overcurly hair, or soft curl perm; medium texture.

Styling Technique

If the hair has received a soft curl perm, apply activator/moisturizer and comb into place. For naturally soft and curly hair, apply a leave-in conditioner and blow dry with diffuser. Using a pick or lift, distribute and pick out hair to desired fullness.

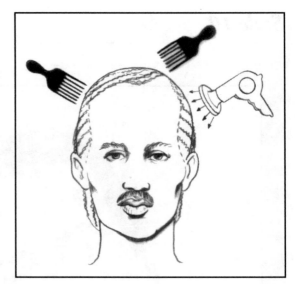

Style 11

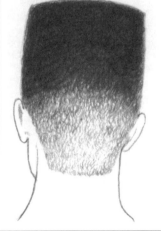

Recommended hair type: Over-curly to natural; thick density, evenly distributed, and/or chemically relaxed hair.

Styling Technique

Apply pink oil or other hairdressing to add sheen and manageability to the hair. Using pick, lift comb, or wide tooth comb, style the hair into its finished form.

Style 12

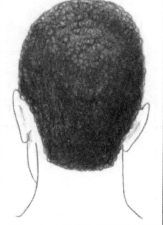

Recommended hair type: Medium texture, over-curly hair; even distribution with no patches, scars, or whorls.

Style 13

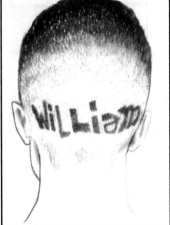

Medium Length (Top) Fade with Optional Signature Design. Recommended hair type: Natural, thick density, evenly distributed.

CUTTING AFRICAN AMERICAN HAIR

Because African American hair is generally very kinky/curly, it's difficult to pull it straight with a comb in order to cut evenly. It's often best to cut this type of hair using a clipper. This is the best way to keep the hair as healthy as possible, free from damaging split ends that may result from too much stress brought on by comb-and-scissor cutting.

BLOW DRYING

Hair styling is the art of arranging hair into an appropriate style following a haircut or shampoo. Many haircuts require minimal styling because of the length of hair, the quality of the cut, and the availability of styling tools like gels, mousses, and hair sprays. Some haircuts, on the other hand, require more styling attention like blow drying or good-old-fashioned finger curling and waving. It's always a good idea to know how to effectively use a variety of techniques in order to create great personal style.

Free-Form Blow-Drying Technique

Free-form blow drying is a quick, easy method of drying hair. It can build fullness into the style and allows the hair to fall into the natural lines of the cut.

Begin at the nape area, holding the hair out of the way with a brush in one hand. As the hair underneath is dried, the brush releases the next area. The dryer should be held six to ten inches from the area being dried, at an angle with the nozzle pointing downward on the hair, and should be moved briskly from side to side as it dries the hair. The sides may be dried in the same manner. The top should be dried loosely and then brushed in to the desired style, followed by the dryer.

Comb-and-Blow-Dryer Technique

After the hair has been shampooed and left damp, apply a styling lotion and comb it through the hair.

1. **Lift along the left hair part.** To create a lift or a little height along the left hair part, start at the front of the head and work toward the crown. Insert the hand comb about one and one-half inches from the part and

draw the comb a little to the back and toward the part simultaneously. This will create a ridge. Adjust the blow dryer to hot and direct the hot air back and forth until a soft ridge has been formed. Repeat, following these instructions, for the second and third sections.

2. **High forward front.** Insert the hand comb from one-half to two inches from the front, depending upon the height of the front hair desired. Draw the comb a little to one side and toward the forehead to create a high ridge. Direct hot air from the blow dryer back and forth along the forehead until a high, soft ridge has been created.

3. **Lift along the right hair part.** Hold the hand comb with the right hand and the blow dryer with the left hand. The procedure is the same as previously outlined for creating a lift for the left side part.

4. **Final steps.** Brush and comb the hair into the desired style.

SHADOW WAVE WITH COMB AND BLOW DRYER

A shadow wave is the same as a regular wave with low ridges. To create it, use a hand comb and blow dryer. Hair that has a natural wave will respond more readily to shadow waving than hair that is straight. Shadow waving is recommended for the front and sides of the head.

1. Shampoo, towel dry, and comb hair in the desired direction. Apply a small amount of styling lotion; add more as needed. Warm water may be used instead of styling lotion.

2. Insert a hand comb about two to two and one-half inches from the hairline and draw the comb forward, a little to one side, so that the hair will form a shallow wave. If the wave does not form readily, the hair can be guided into a wave by pressing it with the index finger or middle finger of the right hand. After the wave has been formed, apply hot air from the blow dryer in a rotating motion. Maintain this position until the wave has formed.

3. After waving, adjust a styling hair net, dry, and finish the hairstyle in the usual manner.

Brush-and-Blow-Dryer Technique

The use of a brush and blow dryer simultaneously is another method of styling the hair. Certain effects, such as wave or ridge formations, smoothing techniques, direction, or volume can be achieved by using various styling brushes. A narrow brush can be used for easier and more precise handling.

Before beginning styling, shampoo and towel dry hair, leaving it damp. Then apply styling lotion, comb through, and proceed with the styling.

CREATE FULLNESS

In areas where fullness is desired, or to give contour to the head, the hair is first lifted with a brush, with hot air from the blow dryer directed at the lifted hair. The hair is then molded softly with the comb or brush into the hairstyle desired.

FULLNESS AT TOP SIDE OF PART

Brush the top hair away from part. Then, with a twist of the wrist, draw the brush slightly toward the part, creating a slight directional ridge. Blow hot air along the ridge, moving the blow dryer back and forth. Avoid blowing hot air on the scalp. Repeat section by section, working from front to back.

FULLNESS ON RIGHT AND LEFT SIDE OF HEAD

To create fullness at the right side of the head, brush the hair slightly toward the back. Then, with a twist of the wrist, turn and push the brush forward, creating a lift. Blow hot air on the area until hair is set in position.

Repeat the same procedure on the left side of the head.

FULLNESS FOR THE FRONT HAIR

A brush may be used to create a high lift at the front hairline. Draw the brush underneath the hair, and with a quick turn of the wrist, turn the brush upward. Use the blow dryer in a back and forth movement until hair is partially dry. Remove the brush by drawing it outward. Then comb so that hair ends blend with the rest of the hairstyle. A shadow wave may be created with the hair ends behind the lifted hair.

CROWN SWIRL

Comb the crown hair in a swirl effect with the grain or in the desired direction. Then brush hair slightly forward in the direction previously followed with the comb. While brushing, twist the wrist inward and draw hair slightly in reverse, thus creating fullness in the area. (Figure 5-14) Blow hot air on the area with a rotating motion until the desired fullness has been achieved. Direct the hot air through hair, avoiding hot air application directly to the scalp. Repeat this procedure on various parts of the crown until the swirl effect has been achieved. To achieve swirl effects on the top and front areas of the head, follow the same procedure. (Figure 5-15)

A finished wave is formed with the air-waver comb and styling comb, taking advantage of the natural waving pattern of hair.

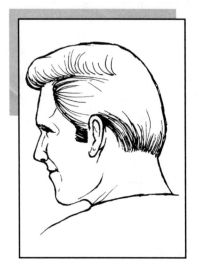

FIGURE 5-14 Swirl fullness in the crown area

FIGURE 5-15 Swirl effects on the top and front areas

AIR CURLING

Air curling is most successful on hair that is naturally curly or has received a permanent wave. The basis for all successful air-curl styling is carefully planned hair cutting. In order to receive air curling properly, hair should be cut with tapered ends. Successful air curling is extremely difficult on hair with blunt-cut hair ends.

The following technique is offered as one method of creating a natural looking, easy-to-wear, informal style with a brush and blow dryer.

Procedure

1. Shampoo and towel dry hair.

2. Apply styling lotion and/or conditioner.

3. Plan the style. Start at the crown or top of the head, as desired. Section the hair, pick up a wide strand, and comb through.

4. Bring the comb out to hair ends and insert the brush. Brush through the strand, bringing the brush out to the ends.

5. Roll hair with the brush, making a complete downward turn, away from the face, until the brush rests on the scalp. Maintain this position and start the blow dryer. Direct the blow dryer very slowly through the curl, using a back-and-forth movement.

6. Continue making curls in the same manner across the crown and back of the head. Clip each curl as completed. Shape the neckline curls with a comb, or make pin curls at the nape for a finished, close-to-the-head look.

In air curling, it's essential that the scalp be thoroughly dry. The hairstyle will not hold if the scalp is damp.

Complete the styling with a light application of lacquer to give shine and holding power to the hair.

FINGER WAVING

Finger waving is the technique of creating a style by using the fingers, a comb, gel, hairpins or clips, and perhaps a hair net. Before you panic about the idea of using hairpins and a hair net, relax. We're not going to make you look like your grandmother. We are, however, going to show you some easy, relatively painless, and thoroughly unembarrassing ways to work with your hair to create a new look.

The best soft, natural waves are obtained in hair that already has a natural or even a permanent wave. Straight hair can be finger waved, but it's a more difficult proposition. As with any other cut or style, the wave should harmonize with the shape of your head as well as with your facial features.

Styling Lotion and Comb

A good styling lotion makes hair pliable and keeps it in place. The proper choice of styling lotion or gel should be governed by the texture and condition of the hair. A good styling lotion is harmless to hair; it should not flake after it has dried.

Hard rubber combs with both fine and coarse teeth are recommended for finger waving.

Preparation

Towel-blot the hair after shampooing. Part the hair, comb it smooth, and arrange it in the desired hairstyle. Apply styling lotion and distribute it with the comb. Avoid using excessive amounts of styling lotion.

To locate the direction of natural hair growth, comb hair away from the face and push it forward with the palm of your hand.

The finger wave may be started on either side of the head. In this presentation, the work begins on the right top side.

Shaping the Top Area

Shape the top hair with a comb, using a circular movement, starting at the front hairline and working toward the back until the crown has been reached.

Forming the First Ridge

1. Place the index finger of the left hand directly above the position for the first ridge.

2. With the teeth of the comb pointing slightly upward, insert the comb directly under the index finger. Draw the comb forward about one inch along the fingertip.

3. With the teeth still inserted in the ridge, flatten the comb against the head in order to hold the ridge in place.

4. Remove the left hand from the head and place the middle finger above the ridge and the index finger on the teeth of the comb. Emphasize the ridge by closing the two fingers and apply pressure. Do not try to increase the height of the ridge by pushing or lifting it up with the fingers. This will distort and move the ridge formation off its base.

5. Without removing the comb, turn the teeth down and comb the hair in a right semicircular motion to form a dip in the hollow part of the wave. This procedure is followed section by section until the crown area has been reached.

6. The ridge and wave of each section should match evenly without showing separations in the ridge and hollow part of the wave.

Forming the Second Ridge

Begin forming the second ridge at the front of the crown area. The movements are the reverse of those followed in forming the first ridge. The comb is drawn back from the fingertip, thus directing the formation of the second ridge. All movements are followed in a reverse pattern until the hairline is reached, thus completing the second ridge. (Figure 5-16)

If an additional ridge is required, the movements are the same as for the first ridge.

FIGURE 5-16 First and second ridge completed

Completing the Finger Wave

1. Place a net over the hair. (Just this once.)

2. Adjust the dryer to medium heat and allow hair to dry thoroughly; otherwise the wave will comb out.

3. After hair is completely dried, remove the hair net. Remove clips and pins from hair.

4. Comb hair into natural waves.

Shadow Waving

Shadow waving is recommended for the sides and sometimes the back of the head. The wave is made in exactly the same manner as a finger wave, except that the ridges are kept low.

Reminders and Hints on Finger Waving

1. Avoid using excessive amounts of styling gels or lotions.
2. Before finger waving, locate the natural wave in hair.
3. To emphasize the ridges of a finger wave, press and close the fingers, holding the ridge against the head.
4. To create a longer-lasting finger wave, mold the waves in the direction of natural hair growth.
5. Before combing, the hair should be thoroughly dried.
6. A styling hair net is placed over hair to protect the setting while hair is being dried.
7. To hold the finger wave in place longer, lightly apply a hair spray.
8. Lightened or tinted hair that tangles or snarls is easier to comb if a conditioner is used.

SAFETY PRECAUTIONS AND REMINDERS

1. Move moderately hot air back and forth on the hair and away from the scalp. Avoid holding the dryer in one place for too long.
2. To avoid scalp burns, keep the teeth of a heated metal comb away from the scalp.
3. Use either hard rubber or metal combs.
4. For best results, hair should be from two to three inches in length.
5. Shampoo hair and leave it slightly damp.
6. If desired, apply a styling gel, lotion, or very warm water before, and sometimes during, the waving.

ACTUAL STYLES AND HOW TO CREATE THEM

You've got a cut that makes the cut. You're feeling good, you're looking better, and now you're really stylin'. Follow these simple ideas to achieve the perfect look for you.

Style 14

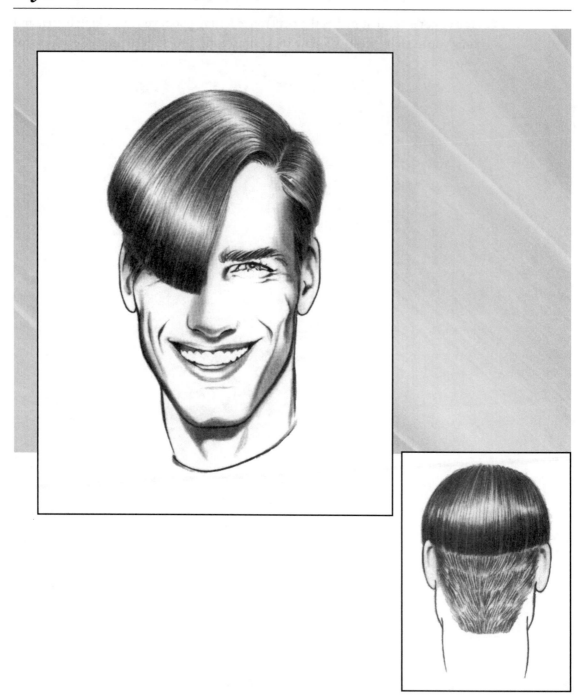

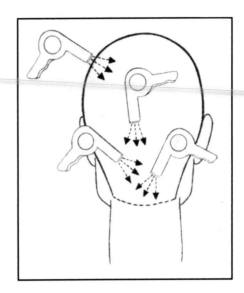

A. Dry hair in the nape and crown area down. At the top of the crown, dry the longer hair diagonally from left to right.

B. Dry the longer hair at the top of right side (light side) diagonally back and up. This will give a spiky effect at the part. Dry the short area diagonally down and back.

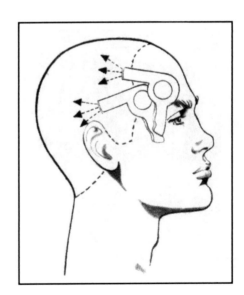

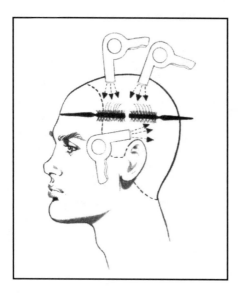

C. Dry the long hair on top across the head from right to left using a vent brush. Turn the ends of the hair under as you dry. Do not try to create volume at the top. Dry the shorter hair diagonally back and down.

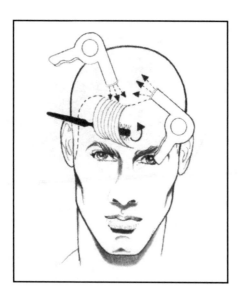

D. Dry the scalp area over the right eye up and back from the face to create height over the right eye. Then dry the ends of the right side and the left side of the bangs under. This will create a wave over the left eye.

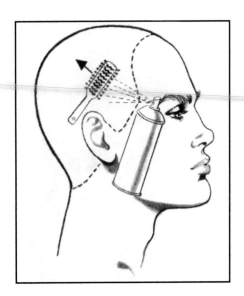

E. Using a vent brush or your fingers, lift hair up on the right side and spray with a strong holding spray.

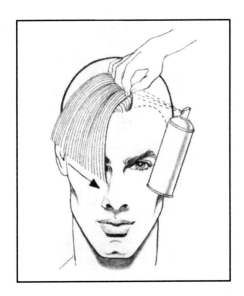

F. Smooth the top and bang section using a comb or brush from right to left. Then take your comb and place at the bottom of the weight line at the back of the head. Run the comb along the weight line towards the face. This will make the line more definite. Using your thumb and index finger, lift a section of hair one inch deep into the hairline over the right eye. Spray the bang with a firm-holding finishing spray.

Style 15

A. Remove most of the moisture from hair before starting to create direction in the blow dry. Start at the perimeter of the nape. Dry the center down and under. Then dry the sides of the perimeter of the nape forward and under. Dry the rest of the hair in the back toward the center, working up to the top of the head. At the top of the back section, dry the hair back.

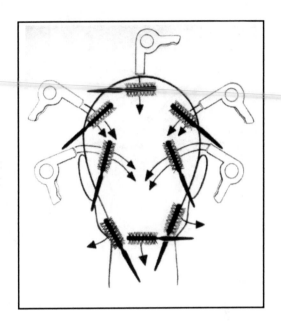

B. On the right side in the perimeter over the ear, dry a section approximately one inch deep straight down and under. Then, starting at the back of the side section, dry the hair diagonally up and back. Work forward to the hairline.

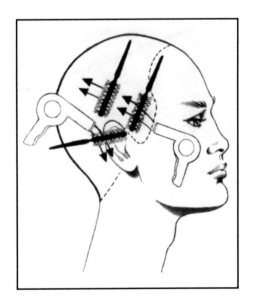

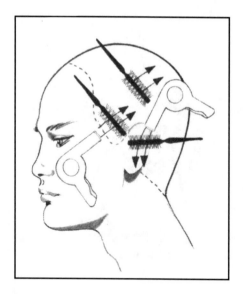

C. Repeat the same procedure on the left side as on the right. Dry the hair over the ear under to give control at the perimeter when combing hair back.

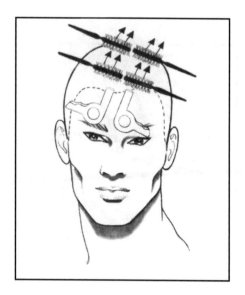

D. Starting at the back of the top section, dry hair diagonally back, lifting the hair away from the head to create some height. Work from the back toward the front hair line. At the hair line, over direct hair back and away from the face.

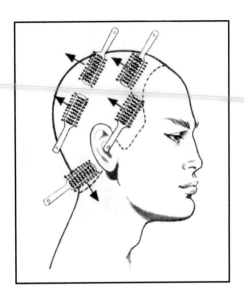

E. Brush the hair in the nape using a vent brush. Turn the hair in the perimeter under in the back. Turn the hair under and toward the front at the sides of the perimeter. Brush the rest of the hair to the center of the back, starting at the nape and working to the top. Brush the sides diagonally back and up. Use long strokes and brush from the hairline all the way to the back.

F. Brush all hair on top at a slight diagonal from right to left. If needed, blend the sides into the top by rebrushing the area between the sides and the top section. Spray with a light-hold finishing spray.

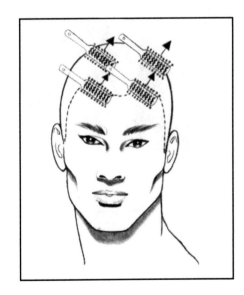

Style 16

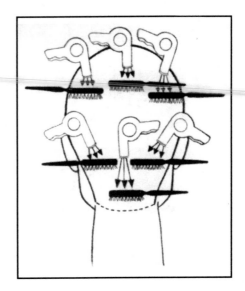

A. Use a blow dryer to dry hair, evenly distributing it across the top of the crown. Dry all hair down, starting in the nape and continuing to the top of the crown.

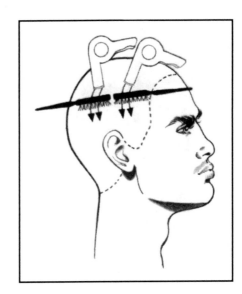

B. On the light side of the part, dry the hair straight down. Start over the ear and work up to the part. Do not lift hair when drying. This style requires hair to be close to the head. Follow through the hair with the dryer after the brush.

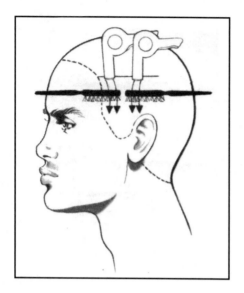

C. Dry the heavy side straight down in the same way as the light side.

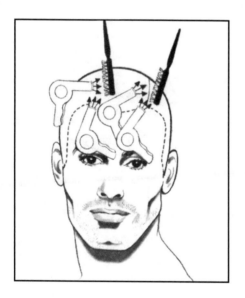

D. Dry the top by brushing across the top section away from the part. Be sure the dryer follows the brush. Start at the back of the top and work forward. If the growth pattern of hair is toward the face, dry hair in the bang section diagonally back.

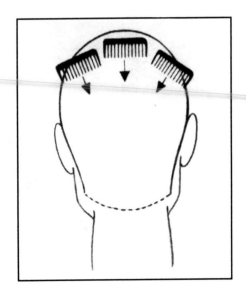

E. Apply a light pomade or styling gel evenly to hair. Use a styling comb to distribute the hair in the crown so it fans out evenly from the center of the crown.

F. Comb the hair on the light side of the part diagonally back and down. Comb the hair on top at the back across the top. Be sure to blend the back of the top section with the top of the crown. Comb the front section of the top diagonally across the head from the part to the heavy side. Finish with a light-holding spray.

Style 17

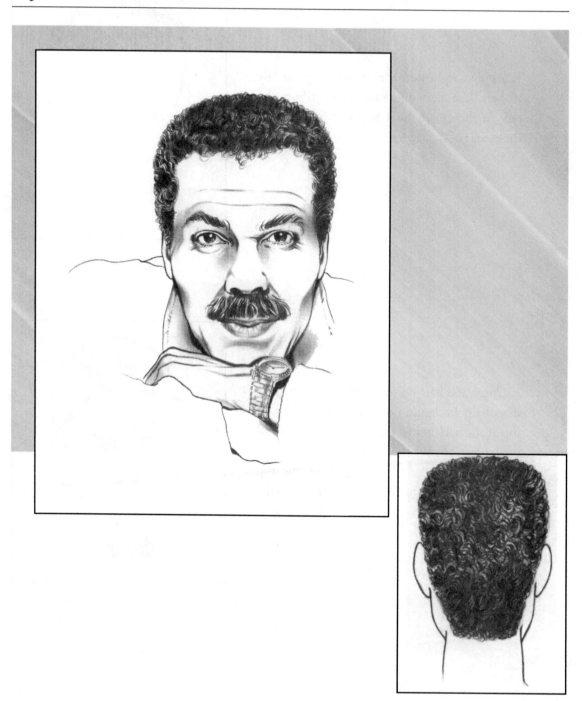

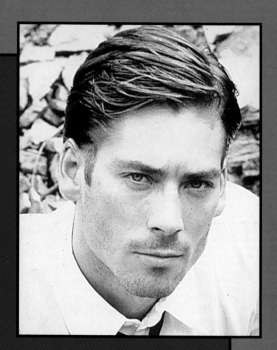

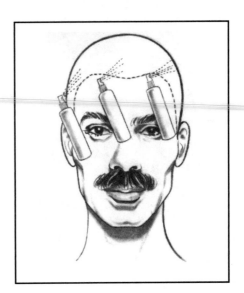

A. Spray your entire head with a soft sculpting spray.

B. Brush hair down in the back.

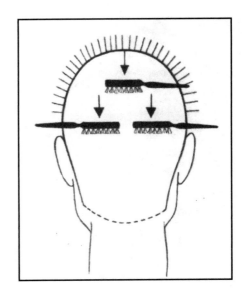

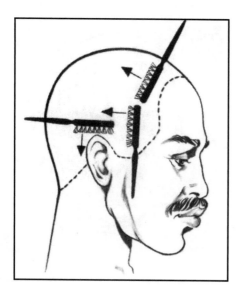

C. Brush hair back on the sides, and down over the ears.

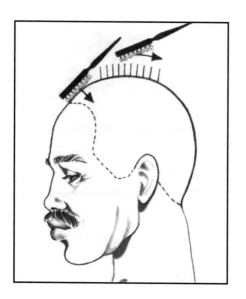

D. Behind the bang section, brush hair straight back. In the longer bang section, brush hair diagonally back and across the head.

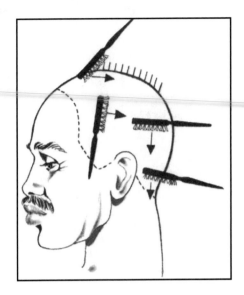

E. After hair has dried, brush it following the same pattern as A through D. This will soften the hair so as not to look like a gel style.

F. Brush the bangs back off the forehead. Use a light pomade on the bangs to help keep them off the face and make hair soft.

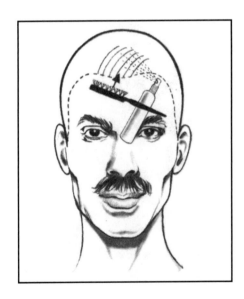

Follicle-ly Challenged

No one can tell exactly when, where, or why hair loss occurs, but, according to the International Society of Hair Restoration Surgery, it affects approximately 35,000,000 men in the United States each year. In fact, twenty percent of men in their twenties suffer from hair loss. Hair loss also affects thirty percent of men in their thirties, forty percent of men in their forties, fifty percent of men in their fifties, and so on. The pattern is clear. This condition is commonly referred to as *male-pattern hair loss,* or MPHL. The politically correct term is *follicle-ly challenged.*

What are some of the theories of hair loss? It might be best first to discuss how hair truly grows. There are three stages of hair growth that result in a loss of about fifty to 200 hairs daily.

1. *Anagen.* This is the growth phase. Hair can grow for as long as six years, depending on your age. As a teenager, you experience a longer anagen stage than when you're older mostly because of hormones.

2. *Catagen.* This is the degradation phase, when the follicle shuts down. This phase lasts for two to three weeks and ends up with a shrunken follicle.

3. *Telogen.* This is the resting phase. The hair has stopped growing completely at this point. The follicle has shrunk, and the mature hair continues to hang on for another two to three months before it falls out. No more than ten percent of your total follicles are in the resting stage at any given time. Once that happens, the process begins again with the anagen stage, unless the follicle dies. Then male pattern hair loss begins.

A number of factors can contribute to the hair growth cycle and cause either temporary or permanent hair loss. These include medication, radiation, chemotherapy, exposure to chemicals, hormonal and nutritional factors, thyroid disease, skin diseases, and even stress.

TEMPORARY HAIR LOSS AND ITS CAUSES

Temporary hair loss occurs for several reasons. The good news is that this type of loss almost always reverses itself and a full head of hair is restored. Some of the causes of temporary hair loss include the following.

- *Stress*—This can be physical stress like fevers, surgery, or anything that affects the body, and emotional stress, or anything that affects the mind.

- *Drugs*—Methamphetamines will cause you to temporarily lose your hair. So will those cortisone shots you get for your bad knee.

- *Diet*—Almost everything behaves badly if you're not eating right and your hair is no exception. Hair needs protein, vitamins, and minerals to grow.

PERMANENT HAIR LOSS AND ITS CAUSES

Permanent hair loss is usually genetic. There's not much you can do about genes unless you can travel back in time, but even then it wouldn't do you much good. You can fight it, but it's really beyond your control.

Genetic hair loss is a direct result of hormones. Testosterone is the most important factor in a male's hair growth. No surprise there. What happens when testosterone accumulates in the blood vessels leading to the growth area of the hair? It overpowers the follicle and kills it. The only thing that can stop this process in genetically inherited MPHL is castration or large doses of the female hormone, estrogen. Because that's probably out of the question, the only thing to do is live with the hair loss or look into transplants. More on that later in this chapter.

Other factors may contribute to permanent hair loss.

- *Not shampooing enough.* An accumulation of scalp debris, often referred to as *dandruff,* oils, dirt, pollution, and styling products suffocates hair follicles, especially when there's too much time between shampoos.

- *Going against the grain.* If you remember, we spoke of hair grain as the natural growth pattern of the hair. When hair is forced to go against that grain, it will—but only for so long. Eventually, the follicle gives in and closes up shop. Pony tail wearers often complain of bald patches. That's because hair is being pulled back and held captive by a band when what it really wants to do is just hang down and be loose. Men who fight their cowlicks and comb, brush, and style against the grain often find themselves suffering from gradually thinning hair. It's hairs' way of saying, "Enough is enough." If you go with the grain, choosing a haircut that accepts your hair's natural position, you'll both be a lot happier in the long run.

- *Malnutrition.* This is something that most people don't realize because they think of hair as being dead. But hair needs as much nutrition to grow as any other part of your body. It needs protein, minerals, and vitamins to stay strong and healthy. If you need evidence of this, look at malnourished people. Their skin is sallow and sagging, and they also suffer from hair loss. While this is a situation that can be reversed, if malnutrition is prolonged, it can lead to permanent hair loss.

You can deal with impending hair loss in a number of ways. One of the more controversial means is scalp massage. A gentle, prodding motion on the scalp turns it from white to a healthier pink because of increased blood flow, which may also help to bring additional nutrients to hair follicles. While this has never been proven, it has not been disproven either. Because it can't hurt, you might want to give it a try.

ANDROGENETIC ALOPECIA

Androgenetic alopecia is the scientific term for male pattern hair loss. *Andro* is the derivative of androgens or males hormones (testosterone, dihydrotestosterone) that produce MPHL. Genetics, as we've already discussed, provides the gene necessary for MPHL to occur. You were born with it, and there's nothing you can do about it, at least not yet.

Androgenetic alopecia is usually noticed first as a receding hair line. In fact, this can be seen in approximately ninety-six percent of white males. Caucasians lead the world in hair loss, with African Americans coming in a close second. It is important to note that a receding hair line does not necessarily mean that you will develop further evidence of MPHL.

Androgens are absolutely necessary in the development of MPHL. The amount does not need to be greater than normal for hair loss to occur. Testosterone is responsible for the growth of what is commonly called *axillary hair,* or underarm and pubic hair. Dihydrotestosterone (DHT) is responsible for beard growth and male pattern hair loss. This is how it works: Testosterone is converted to DHT by an enzyme. Another enzyme, known as *finasteride,* comes in as a blocker, decreasing the amount of DHT. Certain receptors inside cells work to bind androgens, and have a strong attraction to DHT. Once they've pulled DHT inside, this hormone interacts with the nucleus of a cell, altering the production of protein and causing the hair follicle to die.

Men with MPHL experience miniaturized hair shafts, which isn't nearly as painful as it sounds. In fact, it can't be felt at all. When the shafts become smaller and smaller, the outer affected area becomes covered with a very fine form of hair, similar to that which you were born with. Hair color is also affected by this miniaturization. As the shaft shrinks, the pigmentation abilities of the hair are strangled, and the hair becomes very light. These two factors are what causes the first signs of MPHL to appear as thin, or thinning hair.

WOMEN AND HAIR LOSS

If it's any consolation, women also suffer from hair loss, though not as frequently as men. Approximately 21,000,000 women in the United States are affected by female pattern hair loss, or FPHL. This loss becomes particularly noticeable after menopause, when the female hormone estrogen ceases natural production. Women rarely experience the total hair loss that men do, which is fortunate because our society places great value on a woman's "crowning glory."

HAIR TRANSPLANTS

The transplanting of hair is strictly a medical procedure that should be performed only by a trained dermatologist. The process consists of removing hair from normal areas of the scalp, such as the back and sides, and transplanting it into the bald areas. Small sections of hair (about one-eighth of an inch) are surgically removed, including the hair follicle, papilla, and hair bulb, and reset in the bald area. These sections are called *plugs*. A local anesthetic is used. The transplanted hair grows normally in its new environment. The area from which the hair was removed heals and shrinks in size to a very tiny scar.

The dermatologist must select the hair to be transplanted with care, taking into consideration color, texture, and type. Placement of the hair in the direction of natural growth, to permit proper care and grooming, is also an important factor.

Transplanted hair can last a lifetime if the dermatologist service is performed properly. If the doctor is skilled and the individual cares for the hair as directed, hair transplants can be very successful as a method of permanently eliminating baldness.

Hair Weaving

Hair weaving has been practiced in barber shops for many years.

While there are numerous claims of new techniques and exclusive methods in hair weaving, they all follow generally the same procedure. Hair weaving consists of sewing or weaving a foundation into the remaining hair or on the scalp, and then weaving wefts of human hair to this foundation. The two principal techniques are the suture method and the hair-weaving method.

The Suture Method

A perimeter of anchor bases, made of strong, non-reactive, teflon coated, stainless steel wire, is imbedded or sutured into the scalp by a medical doctor. To this imbedded wire, a foundation of siliconized Dacron is attached. This foundation must fit the scalp very tightly and snugly. Wefts of matching human hair are sewn or woven to the foundation in a previously determined pattern and style. Since the foundation wires are imbedded in the scalp, the suture method of hair weaving is not affected by hair growth.

While the suture method seems to offer a hair replacement technique involving some semblance of permanency without constant adjustments, it also presents a number of severe problems. These include the danger of scalp infection from the teflon wire, the possibility of pain when combing or shampooing the hair, and the danger of injury to the scalp caused by pulling the wire in combing. Clients should be advised to consider carefully all possible complications before deciding upon this form of hair replacement.

THE HAIR-WEAVING METHOD

This method consists of firmly sewing or weaving a foundation into the remaining hair on the individual's head with thread and then sewing or weaving wefts of matching human hair to the foundation in a pre-planned pattern. Since the foundation is attached to the remaining hair on the head, as the hair grows the foundation moves out from the scalp. Continual adjustments are required in order to maintain the desired natural appearance.

The woven hair requires continuous care and servicing. The foundation must be tightened and brought close to the scalp every six to eight weeks.

The hair must be shampooed carefully, in sections, to avoid pulling and causing damage to the foundation or pain. Hair should also receive periodic conditioning treatments to add luster and to avoid dryness and damage.

HAIRPIECES

The quality of a hairpiece varies with the kind of hair it contains, the way it's constructed, and how it's fitted.

Types of Hair

Human hair is the most desirable choice for a quality hairpiece. The hairpieces most commonly available are made of Caucasian and Oriental hair. First-quality human hair is usually in a virgin condition, thereby assuring minimal oxidation. Oriental hair has many good qualities. However, the usual straight, coarse texture and dark color often require waving and/or coloring in order to match the client's hair. This processing diminishes the strength of the hair and oxidation occurs when the hair is exposed to sunlight and natural elements.

Animal hair, usually angora or yak, is used in the manufacture of hairpieces. Angora has a finer texture than yak and is often used at the front hairline to create a softer, more natural look.

Synthetic hair is used primarily in the production of full wigs, rather than pieces. It's difficult to match the texture of synthetic hair with human hair, which makes blending difficult. Synthetic fibers also possess a high gloss, which makes them more noticeable. The positive factors of synthetics are that the fibers will not oxidize or lose the style. The continuing research of synthetic fibers may eventually result in the production of a hairpiece fiber equal in quality to that of human hair.

Hairpieces constructed of synthetic hair or a blend of human and synthetic or animal hair have the following disadvantages.

- They're difficult to handle, tending to mat and tangle easily.
- They're stiff and have a glassy surface shine.
- Human hair shades cannot be duplicated readily.

Because most of the hair used in hairpieces is imported, it must be prepared for use. The usual process includes these steps.

1. chemically cleaning the hair with an acid solution
2. sorting the hair by color and length
3. aligning or root-turning the hair, meaning that all the hair is turned in the same direction as it would grow on the head
4. giving the hair a permatizing bath

Bases and Construction

Hairpieces are available with hard, soft, net, plastic, or combination bases. The types of construction include the following.

- wefted—machine made
- handmade—usually ventilated
- ventilated—with lace front
- hard base

Stock and Custom Hairpieces

Hairpieces are available from manufacturers and distributors in stock sizes and colors. Your stylist maintains an inventory of these products. Custom hairpieces, however, require that the stylist measure your balding area to create a pattern for the supplier to use as a guide in the production of the hairpiece.

Before you invest in a hairpiece, have a pattern or contour analysis done. The contour analysis will help to determine whether a hairpiece is suitable for you.

Implements and Supplies Used for Men's Hairpieces

Most of the implements and supplies required for men's hairpiece services are available in a barber-styling shop. The remainder can be obtained easily from a supply company.

MEASURING FOR A HAIRPIECE

Preliminary Haircut

To achieve a natural look, your hair should be allowed to grow fairly long, thus making it much easier to blend with that of the hairpiece. When your hair is cut, it should be trimmed very lightly. The neckline should be low and hair should be kept close to the ears at the sides.

Tape Measurement

For a front hairline to look natural, it should not be too low on the forehead. The original natural hairline should be followed as closely as possible. The stylist will place three fingers above the eyebrow, directly in line with the center of the nose, and make a dot with a grease pencil on the forehead to indicate where the hairpiece is to begin. (Figure 6-1) Using a tape, the stylist measures from the dot to where the back hair begins and marks the tape measure. (Figure 6-2)

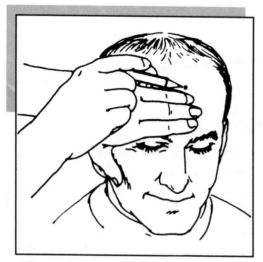

FIGURE 6-1   The stylist indicates where the hairpiece will begin

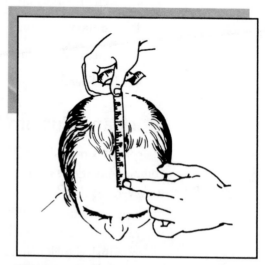

FIGURE 6-2   Measuring from front to where the back hair begins

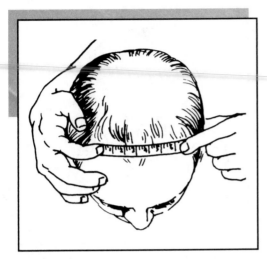

FIGURE 6-3   Measuring across the top

The next measurement is across the top, directly over the sideburn (normally about one and one-half inches behind the forehead dot). This is the place where the front hairline of the head piece blends in with the hair at the sides of the head. (Figure 6-3)

Manufacturer's Code

The sizes of men's hairpieces are commonly referred to by these measurements. For example: a six-by-four-inch piece would be six inches long from front to back, and four inches wide. The larger number refers to the length unless otherwise indicated.

Pattern Measurements

Tape measurements alone can be used by experienced designers in most cases. In some instances, a pattern may be preferable. The stylist places plastic wrap on top of your individual's head and twists the sides until they conform to the contour of the head. While you hold the plastic wrap, the stylist places pre-cut strips of tape across the bald area to stiffen the pattern and hold its shape. (Figures 6-4 and 6-5)

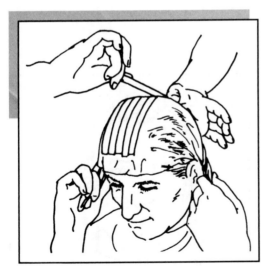

FIGURE 6-4   Using plastic wrap and tape, the stylist makes a pattern

The balding area is then outlined on the pattern as follows. Two dots are placed on each side where the front hairline is to meet your hairline. Two dots are placed in back of the head on each side of the balding spot. And one dot is placed at the center back edge of the bald spot to determine the length of the area to be covered. The dots are then connected with a pencil to outline the balding area. (Figures 6-6 through 6-8)

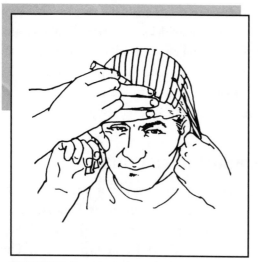

FIGURE 6-5 The stylist indicates the new hairline on the pattern

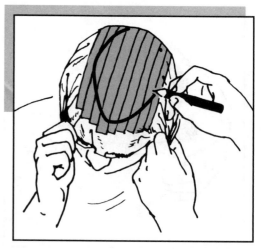

FIGURE 6-6 The stylist outlines the balding area on the pattern

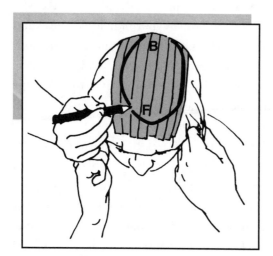

FIGURE 6-7 The stylist marks the front and back parts of the pattern

FIGURE 6-8 The stylist replaces the cut pattern over the balding area

Another method for taking a pattern is with a plaster-cast type material. Some hairpiece manufacturers prefer this method because it gives a true-to-shape form of the bald area. This is the same material used in setting broken bones.

Hair Samples

For a hairpiece to look natural, the stylist should take samples of your hair so that it can be matched by the manufacturer.

Applying Hairpiece

Before adjusting a hairpiece to your scalp, clean the entire bald area with a piece of cotton dampened with rubbing alcohol or soap and water. Then dry thoroughly.

Place two-sided tape in a V-shape on the front reinforced area of the foundation. (Figure 6-9) This tape holds the hairpiece close to the scalp.

Place additional pieces of tape on the reinforced parts of the foundation at the sides and back of the hairpiece.

Place three fingers above the eyebrow, thus locating the hairline (Figure 6-10); position the hairpiece at the hairline using the center of the nose as a guide. When the hairpiece is in proper position, press down firmly on the various tape areas. (Figure 6-11)

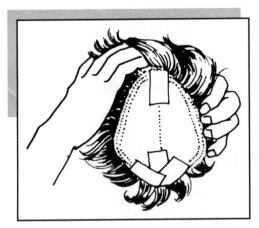

FIGURE 6-9   Place tape on the foundation as shown

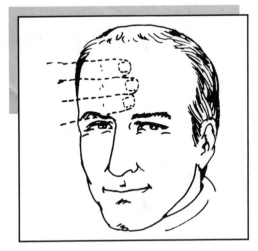

FIGURE 6-10   Locate the hairline

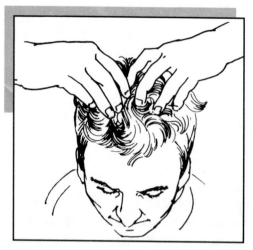

FIGURE 6-11 Position and secure the hairpiece

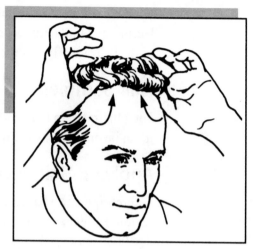

FIGURE 6-12 Remove tape from the scalp

Cutting, Tapering, and Blending

After combing the hair into the desired position, the stylist will taper and blend the hair smoothly at the back and sides of the head so that the hairpiece will be undetectable from your hair.

Removing a Hairpiece

Reach up under the hairpiece with the fingertips and detach the tape from the scalp. (Figure 6-12) Make sure the tape stays on the foundation. This tape is left on the foundation, and it is reactivated with spirit gum or nail polish remover each time the hairpiece is worn.

PUTTING ON AND STYLING A HAIRPIECE WITH A LACE FRONT

A hairpiece with a lace front is recommended when the hair is worn in an off-the-face style. It is scarcely visible from the front view. The use of a lace-front hairpiece gives the required lightness for a natural-looking hairstyle. This natural effect is impossible to achieve with other types of hairpieces.

Putting on a Hairpiece

1. Clean the bald area with rubbing alcohol or with soap and water.

2. Remove hair on the scalp where the tape or lace is to be attached.

3. Attach strips of tape (two-sided) to reinforced parts of the foundation, usually near front, on the sides, and the back part of the hairpiece. (Figure 6-13) Reinforced areas vary with the design of the foundation and the manufacturer's specifications.

4. Adjust the hairpiece to the desired position using the three-finger method previously described. Press it down into place.

FIGURE 6-13   Apply tape to reinforced areas

CAUTION!   *Never use tape directly on the lace.*

The stylist will cut, taper, and blend the front lace hairpiece to match smoothly with your hair. The lace will be trimmed to within one-quarter of an inch of the hairline or right down to the contour of the hairline, according to your preference. The decision to trim or not to trim should be left until the hairpiece has been worn for a while. In the beginning, leave a small, one-quarter inch margin.

Removing a Lace-Front Hairpiece

1. Before removing a lace-front hairpiece, dampen the lace with acetone or solvent in order to loosen it from the scalp. Do not pull or stretch the lace. To apply solvent, use a piece of cotton or a brush.

2. After the lace becomes loosened, use the fingertips to remove the tape from the scalp. (Figure 6-14) Do not pull off the hairpiece by tugging on the hair.

3. The pieces of tape are not removed from the reinforced areas of the hairpiece. They are reactivated with spirit gum or nail polish remover each time the hairpiece is worn.

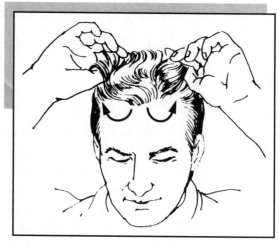

FIGURE 6-14   Remove tape from the scalp

PARTIAL HAIRPIECES

Partial Lace Front Fill-In

For a small degree of hair loss, a partial lace fill-in may be all that is required.

1. Clean the area with soap and water or with rubbing alcohol and allow it to dry. Brush on spirit gum and wait until it gets tacky.

2. Place the hairpiece properly and press down.

3. Comb into the rest of the hair. If necessary, have the stylist taper and shorten the hairpiece to blend in with your hair.

Frontal lace partials are made of very fine lace, and they are excellent for receding hairpart lines.

Partial Crown Hairpiece

For those who are bald at the crown, a small hairpiece may be used. To attach a partial crown, clean the area in the usual manner, dry, and apply spirit gum to the outer edges of the bald spot. Then do the following.

1. Attach a piece of two-sided tape to the center of the hairpiece.

2. Carefully position the hairpiece over the bald spot, press the center firmly to the scalp, and then press the outer edges into position. Once in position, it may be held in place with two-sided adhesive tape or spirit gum.

3. Have the stylist cut, taper, and blend the hairpiece with your hair.

CLEANING AND STYLING HAIRPIECES

Cleaning Hairpieces

Great care should be taken when cleaning hairpieces. Remove all old tape (Figure 6-15) and clean any reinforced areas by rubbing them lightly with solvent or wig cleaner.

Put enough cleaner in an open bowl so that the hairpiece can be submerged. Swish the hairpiece back and forth (or dip it up and down) in the cleaner until all residue is removed from the hair and foundation. Gently press out the cleaner or let it drip into the bowl. Fasten the hairpiece on a covered head mold to dry naturally.

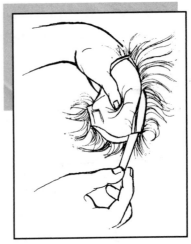

FIGURE 6-15 Remove tape before cleaning

CAUTION! *Some cleaning agents are hazardous if not used according to instructions. Be sure to read the label carefully before using any cleaning agent.*

Cleaning Synthetic Hairpieces

Synthetic hairpieces should never be washed in solvent. Attach the hairpiece to a styrofoam head mold with T-pins. Then immerse it in lukewarm water with a mild shampoo. Do not use hot water or the hairpiece will shrink. Swish the hairpiece around in the shampoo solution. Rinse with clean, lukewarm water. Allow the hairpiece to dry naturally, pinned on the mold overnight. If time doesn't permit place it under a dryer with cool air. Some hairpieces may be dry cleaned. Follow the manufacturer's instructions.

Special Note About Hairpieces

Hairpieces made of human hair must always be dry cleaned. Never use a shampoo. Follow the manufacturer's recommendations.

Synthetic hairpieces are usually mass-produced and generally have a coarser texture than human hair hairpieces. Because synthetic fibers are rarely used for lace-type or custom-made hairpieces, the differences between synthetic fiber and human hair hairpieces are usually discernable.

CHAPTER 7

Color: It's Not Just for Women

We were born with a particular type of hair. It was thick and dark, or thin and blonde. Sometimes it was straight, sometimes curly, occasionally it had a simple wave. It turned gray as we aged, got more wiry, and eventually fell out. But this story has a happy ending. We can change whatever kind of hair we were genetically dealt. We have the technology. No longer do we have to be satisfied with our dark hair when we wish we were blonde. We don't have to accept aging with grace and dignity. Get out the hair color and—presto! Instant youth!

Hair color in the United States accounts for billions of dollars fed into the economy every year. Just take a walk down the hair care aisles at your local grocery or drug store to witness shelf upon shelf stacked with hair color products. Some are permanent, some are semi-permanent, still others tout themselves as demi-permanent. How do you know what to choose?

It would be easy to say that the decision is completely up to you, and for the most part, it is. No one can decide whether coloring your hair is right for you except you. The one thing that you can keep in mind, however, is that hair color is not just for women anymore. Men all over the country are coloring their hair and having fun at the same time.

TEMPORARY HAIR COLOR

These colors are made up of pigment and large dye molecules. This means that they are unable to penetrate into the cuticle layer of hair, thereby making only a physical change as opposed to a chemical change. In essence, the color coats the hair shaft, depositing new color but not changing the natural color. These types of colors can be removed as early as the next shampoo and are not generally recommended for someone who wants to get rid of gray.

Types of temporary haircoloring include the following.

1. *Color rinses*—These contain certified colors that highlight existing color. They're designed to wash out with the next shampoo.

2. *Highlighting color shampoos*—These combine the action of a color rinse with the cleansing action of a shampoo, giving highlights and showcasing color tones already present in hair.

3. *Crayons*—You've most likely seen these types of color as highlighting sticks that can temporarily color a moustache. They come in several colors, ranging from blonde to auburn to black, and are a great way to retouch gray or white "roots" between coloring.

4. *Hair color sprays*—This is a party in a can. Spray the color onto dry hair and go out for the night.

5. *Hair color mousses*—Another party in a can. These are perfect for adding just a touch of fun to your style. They wash out with shampoo.

Use a temporary color to bring out highlights in hair of any shade, to temporarily restore faded hair to its natural shade, to neutralize the yellowish tinge in white or gray hair, and to tone down over-lightened, or bleached, hair.

To apply a color rinse, follow the manufacturer's directions.

Semi-permanent Hair Color

For a slight change in color that lasts about four weeks, consider semi-permanent colors. These deposit color in the cortical layer of hair and coat the hair shaft at the same time. Regarded as self-penetrating because of the direct dyes that are used, semi-permanent colors do not have to be mixed with hydrogen peroxide or other color developers. However, they cannot lighten natural hair color and cover gray hair for only a short period of time.

Demi-permanent hair color is very similar to semi-permanent. The color dyes are a bit stronger and stain the hair for a bit longer, but they still do not alter the chemical makeup of each individual hair.

Semi- and demi-permanent colors can be described in these ways.

1. They do not require the addition of hydrogen peroxide.

2. The color is self-penetrating.

3. The color is applied the same way each time.

4. Retouching is eliminated.

5. Color does not rub off because it has penetrated the hair shaft slightly.

6. Hair will return to its natural color in four to six weeks.

To apply semi-permanent hair color, follow the manufacturer's directions.

To truly change your hair color, you must venture into the realm of permanent hair color.

PERMANENT HAIR COLOR

Permanent hair colors are designed to alter the chemistry of hair. The dyes used require a color developer like hydrogen peroxide to open the cuticle and lay a new color inside. Because of this action, permanent colors can both lift existing color and deposit new color. Permanent colors do not wash out, but they do grow out. Depending on how fast your hair grows, you'll start to see "roots" after about four weeks. This represents new hair growth, or hair that hasn't been colored. As your hair continues to grow, your roots will become longer. If you've used a permanent color, you can easily retouch this new growth by applying color only to the roots.

Your hairstylist or barber is well versed in coloring techniques and can help you achieve the color you desire. However, if you choose to color your hair yourself, in the privacy of your own bathroom, simply follow the manufacturer's directions. It's fairly quick and relatively painless. The only thing that you'll experience is a slight tingling/burning sensation on your scalp when you initially apply the color. This is the result of the hydrogen peroxide or color developer. It leaves no residual damage and usually goes away within three to five minutes.

Permanent hair colors fall into four categories.

1. *Oxidation tints*—These tints can lighten and deposit color in a single process and are available in a wide variety of colors. If you're using an over-the-counter brand, check the box. If you're having color done in a

salon, talk to your stylist about what shade you wish to achieve. Because of their advanced training in color theory, stylists can mix colors to achieve your desired result. Oxidation tints are sold in bottles and tubes, in either semi-liquid or cream form. They must be mixed with hydrogen peroxide to produce the chemical reaction known as *oxidation*. This reaction begins as soon as the two compounds are mixed, so color must be applied immediately. Any leftover should be discarded immediately.

2. *Vegetable tints*—These colors are made from various plants, herbs, and flowers. Certain types are standards, like indigo, chamomile, sage, and Egyptian henna. Henna is still used as a professional hair color, but it can over-coat the hair, causing build-up and preventing the penetration of other chemicals, leaving hair unfit for other chemical treatments.

3. *Metallic or mineral dyes*—These are sometimes advertised as "progressive colors." However, metallic ingredients like lead acetate or silver nitrate often react with the keratin in hair, turning it brown and leaving a dull, metallic appearance. (Visualize pennies that need to be polished.) Repeated applications can damage the hair.

4. *Compound dyes*—These are metallic or mineral dyes combined with vegetable tints. They give the color more staying power and can create a myriad of different colors, but are generally not used professionally.

For permanent color application, carefully read and follow the manufacturer's directions.

DECOLORING OR BLEACHING

Simply put, bleach lifts color from the hair without depositing another color in its place, thus leaving the hair naked. Professionally referred to as *lighteners,* bleaches use hydrogen peroxide along with a specific bleaching formula to create a chemical heat. This heat opens the cuticle and blasts out the color. Don't worry: it's not painful.

Hair goes through seven stages of lightening from the darkest to the lightest. For example, natural black hair will go from black to brown, to red, to red-gold, to gold, to yellow, and finally to pale yellow.

Bleaches or hair lighteners can be used in the following ways.

- to lighten the entire head of hair
- to lighten the hair to a particular shade
- to brighten and lighten an existing shade
- to tip or streak certain parts of the hair
- to lighten hair that has already been tinted
- to remove undesirable shades
- to correct dark streaks or spots in hair that has already been lightened or tinted

Bleaching is something that should be done in a salon or in a controlled environment to ensure the best results. If you do it at home, be sure to carefully read and follow the manufacturer's directions.

WHY COLOR AT ALL?

Naturally, choosing to change your hair color is a decision that you must make for yourself. But with the amazing color and phenomenal results achieved with today's colors, the real question becomes "Why *not* color?"

It's fun. And even with permanent color, it won't last forever.

Chemical Services

Curly hair can now be straightened, permanently or temporarily. Straight hair can be curled. It's a mad, mad, mad, mad world. But it sure is fun.

PERMS

If done correctly, perms can increase the fullness of fine, soft hair, redirect resistant growth patterns (like cowlicks), restructure straight hair into waves or curls, and provide greater styling control. That's the good news. Here's the bad: They can also torture hair beyond the limits of human dignity, and leave behind frazzled, finger-in-the-socket frizz.

Permanent waves aren't permanent. As long as the hair continues to grow, a perm will eventually grow out. Perms also cause the most amount of damage to hair, next to relaxers. Sections of hair are tightly wrapped around a rod—the number of sections and the size of the rod depend on how much and how big the desired curl—and a high pH chemical solution that changes the cellular structure of the hair is applied. After a prescribed period of time, a neutralizer is applied to stop the action.

A perm damages the cuticle layer so that hair tangles more easily. It can also contribute to breakage. Hair can be left dull with major split ends.

But perms do have their advantages. Guys with hair that's fine, straight, and limp want more body and fullness, just like anybody else. And since you're not apt to hang around the house with curlers in your hair, getting a body wave might not be a bad idea.

Before you proceed, either at home or at the salon, keep these things in mind.

1. A perm should never be given to hair that has already had a perm and has remnants of that perm still visible. When you apply a new perm over an old perm, you're asking for trouble with a capital "D." Damage control will soon follow, and it will all result in more trouble than it's worth.

2. Never brush out permed hair that is still wet. Use a comb or brush with wide-spaced teeth to help untangle your newly acquired mass of curls.

3. Try not to use a blow dryer, especially on a curly perm. You might end up with more frizz than you bargained for.

If you're going to perm at home, follow the manufacturer's directions carefully.

RELAXERS

Relaxers offer the opposite of a perm. Used to remove curl and wave, this chemical reaction can cause just as much damage as a perm because it uses similar technology. A chemical relaxer is pulled through the hair and left on for a predetermined amount of time before being neutralized. The result is straight hair that can also suffer from dullness and breakage. Relaxed hair, like permed hair, is very fragile and must be treated with deep conditioners and remoisturizers.

While you can purchase a number of reactive, chemical-free straighteners that provide temporary straightening effects, a relaxer is always applied at a salon. See your hairstylist or barber for this procedure.

General Grooming

BASIC SKIN CARE AND FEEDING

The first thing to know about your skin is that it is a living organ, but that it doesn't breathe. It does, however, nourish itself with oxygen and other nutrients that circulate through the blood. Oxygen enters skin cells, though not through the outer layer of the skin. The skin then expels toxins, sweat, and oils through its pores, and all of this can clog pores and make it seem as if the skin is choking.

The Things Skin Can Tell

Skin also reveals a lot about what the body may be lacking in essential nutrients. For example, ugly skin lesions are a symptom of a disease called *scurvy,* caused by a lack of vitamin C. A characteristic skin rash that can cause scarring indicates a disease called *pellagra,* which is the result of a severe vitamin B deficiency. Other skin disorders that can have a nutritional origin are acne, eczema, psoriasis, and dermatitis (a skin inflammation).

What can you do for your skin other than eat more fruits and vegetables and cut down on alcohol consumption and smoking? Give your skin a proper, thorough cleansing.

Begin with Cleansing

A simple wash will help remove debris from your skin's surface and restore its ability to replenish, rejuvenate, and renourish itself. Skin care doesn't have to be complicated or expensive, but it does have to be consistent. Always wash your face with lukewarm water. Because the vascular system of the face consists of tiny capillaries—capillaries that are, by nature, extremely weak—exposure to extreme temperatures can cause them to break. Broken capillaries are highly visible underneath the skin, leading to redness and sensitivity. The best way to keep from causing this type of damage to your face is to cup your hands and splash moderately warm water on your face. Never turn your face directly into hot water. While it may feel good, it won't look good for long.

It's also a good idea to avoid cold water, even though it, too, might feel great after a hot day. Also keep shampoo and other hair products away from your face because some of the ingredients used for hair care may irritate your face.

And always remember your neck. It should be part of your face care regimen for two reasons: (1) It is one of those telling areas that show age, and (2) it responds very well to care.

Skin care is quite often a matter of trial and error. "Hypoallergenic," "allergy-free," and "dermatologist-tested" are strong buzzwords, but it is important to know that there are currently no guidelines set by the Food and Drug Administration (FDA) in defining product categories. Products that carry these terms may be less likely to cause an allergic reaction. And, yes, any product carrying one of these terms has been tested by a dermatologist or skin specialist. But regardless of package claims, you'll still have to try a product out for yourself to see if it works on your skin.

Whatever type of product you choose, from lightweight moisturizing lotions to heavier creams that target specific skin areas (for example, eyes or throat), from refreshing toners to pore-cleansing masks, be sure to test it on a small area of skin first. Once you're satisfied that what you've chosen is good on your skin (you'll find out about what makes it good for your skin later), establish a regimen and stick to it. It's as easy as 1, 2, 3.

Skin Care Regimen: 1, 2, 3

1. CLEANSING

Cleansers help to remove oil, dirt, sweat, and debris from the surface of skin. Cleansers can be as simple as a bar of moisturizing soap or as complex as a scrub. Soaps contain detergents and foaming agents that are instrumental in giving skin that "squeaky clean" feeling. Scrubs can contain more exotic ingredients including herbs and organic botanicals that combine to do just as the product says: "scrub" skin.

One of the common misconceptions about cleansers is that they are moisturizers. While some may contain moisturizing ingredients that keep skin feeling soft and smooth even after cleansing, they are no substitute for a true moisturizer. A moisturizer's primary function is to rehydrate skin, and it is left on the skin after application. A cleanser, in contrast, is applied and then removed completely. The best kinds of cleansers, those that are perfect for your skin, will wash away completely, leaving nothing on your skin but the faintest of fragrances.

Cleansing is one of the most important things you can do for your skin because everything else that you do follows. Cleansing will return your skin to its most natural state, maintaining the health and vitality of the pores. This is especially important because clogged pores lead to blemishes and acne.

Like an artist preparing a canvas, you must prepare your face for the art to follow. To do this, you must begin with a cleanser that is acidic, or nonalkaline. That's because your skin is naturally acidic. Alkaline products shouldn't be used, because they will strip your skin of natural oils. The pH level of a product will tell you how acidic or alkaline that product is. Generally your skin falls within the 5.0 to 6.0 pH range. So the ideal pH of your cleanser should be around 5.0. If the pH of a skin care product is not listed, you can test it yourself. Take a trip to your local pharmacy and purchase nitrazine papers. You can dip one right into the jar or bottle of your cleanser as a test. Or you can pour a little of the product onto the strip to see if it is acidic or alkaline. Keep in mind that you want acidic products.

Once you've found a cleanser that's the proper pH, start using it in the morning and especially at night to remove makeup as well as the dirt of the day. Non-moisturizing or body soaps actually get skin too clean, stripping away too much of its natural oils, so a cleanser is usually your best bet.

What's the best way to cleanse? Pour your chosen cleanser into the palms of your hands, rub your palms together, and gently apply the cleanser to your face and neck. Be sure not to rub too hard. Your skin may not be as fragile as an egg, but there's nothing wrong with treating it as such. You can use a washcloth if you like, but hands are generally the best tools for helping to dislodge surface debris. Using your hands also gets you used to the feel of your skin so you'll know exactly when you're done and ready to move on.

Follow the manufacturer's directions when using the cleanser, adding a bit of water if you think it's too dry. Spread the cleanser across your skin, massaging gently, and then rinse using lukewarm water. Rinse as many times as necessary to remove all traces of dirt and oils as well as the cleansing product. Makeup can be especially hard to remove, so you might want to think about cleansing twice to make sure that your skin is as clean as possible.

Once all the cleanser is gone, you're ready to begin the next step in your regimen: toning.

2. TONING

A toner is one of the most important parts of your daily regimen. Toners are astringents, or fresheners, that work to clarify and tone skin after cleansing. They aren't cleansers. While some toners may tell you to use them to remove excess oils and dirt, if your skin isn't clean, you should go back to the cleanser.

In addition to making skin feel tighter, toners prepare the skin for moisturizers. Because they are primarily made up of water, toners will also make your skin feel more hydrated after cleansing, but they are not replacements for moisturizers either.

The tightening feeling that you often experience after toning is caused by the alcohol present in most toners. Alcohol, applied directly to freshly cleansed skin, causes skin to swell slightly, which makes it feel tighter. But it's important to remember that toners do not change the physical structure of skin in any way.

When choosing a toner, look closely at the ingredients. Stay away from toners containing SD, ethyl, or isopropyl alcohol. These are very drying and tend to encourage unhealthy skin. Cetyl alcohol, in comparison, is used in many cosmetics and isn't harmful to the skin.

You may think that oily skin needs a toner with a very drying alcohol in order to help control the release of natural oil, but what more commonly happens is that the skin begins to suffer from dehydration. The reason is that the alcohol doesn't stop the oil glands from producing oils; instead it just works to dry up the existing surface oils. This leaves the skin unbalanced and can actually cause the oil glands to produce more oil to compensate. So what you're likely to be left with is skin that is oilier than when you started. No fun at all.

The list of ingredients on the ideal toning product will be short. The more chemicals on the list, the more chances there are for skin irritation and flare-ups. What you do want to see on the list is water, and it should be the first ingredient listed. (Ingredients are listed from most to least, so if water is listed first, there is more water in the toner than any other ingredient.) Also make note of the fragrance. Choose a toner that smells good and isn't overpowering since you'll be able to smell it when it's on your skin. Natural oils like lavender are the best because they're also naturally acidic and won't dry out your skin.

Toners do not need to be wiped on or off. Let's say that again: Toners don't need to be wiped on or off. The old days of taking a cotton ball, drenching it with toner, and swiping across your skin are long gone. The new way of applying toner is to spray it on. Since the idea of a toner is to refresh and invigorate your skin, a light mist will do wonders for making your cleansed skin look and feel great. And if the toner you choose doesn't come with a spray bottle, you can always pick up an empty one at your stylist's shop, pharmacy, or grocery store.

Remember to always use your toner after you've cleansed your face. This will create the right environment for applying a moisturizer.

3. MOISTURIZING

Always apply moisturizers after cleansing and toning. Moisturizers come in the form of creams and lotions, and sometimes even a hydrating gel that glides over cleansed and toned facial skin to soften and smooth. Usually consisting of an emollient in water, moisturizers work to protect your delicate skin from the damaging environment. By adding a fine layer of hydration, moisturizers give the appearance of reducing fine lines and wrinkles. They don't actually repair or erase these signs of age, but they do help. They also help to smooth skin, which is especially important for people with dry skin. If you suffer from dry skin, you understand what it means to have skin that feels chalky or dusty. This comes from a marked lack of natural oil in the skin. A good moisturizer will help make up for what you weren't born with.

People with oilier skin, in comparison, usually feel as if they have an abundance of natural moisture. If you have oily skin, you probably wonder if you need a moisturizer at all. The answer is yes. Everyone needs a moisturizer, even people with oily skin. Why? Chances are, if you have oily skin, you spend a great deal of time trying to get rid of the oil with products that may have a tendency to dry out your skin. The alcohol-based toners we discussed in Step 2 are a good example. As we already noted, these types of toners can cause skin irritation. If you do use an alcohol-based toner, moisturizers will help to soothe and smooth away that irritation.

If you do have oily skin and feel very strongly about not using a moisturizer, the choice is yours. However, without a moisturizer, you leave your skin exposed to additional environmental damage. You might try a gel-based moisturizer because it is usually lighter in weight and feel than creams and lotions, and seems to be absorbed more quickly into the skin.

Be sure to always use a nonalkaline cream, lotion, or gel when choosing a moisturizer, and choose one based on its consistency. Drier skin types will benefit more from a heavier moisturizer, and oily skin types will fare better with a lightweight hydrator.

Most moisturizers will be labeled for a particular skin type. The common descriptors are "normal to dry" and "normal to oily/combination." Some moisturizers even claim to be oil-free. While they may not contain any oils per se, they might contain other emollient ingredients that can also clog the pores.

There is another dilemma that faces moisturizer users, and that is whether it's important to have different moisturizers for daytime and nighttime use. The answer is yes—and no.

Day creams tend to be a bit lighter and add that all-important protective layer between skin and environmental factors. Many day moisturizers also contain a sunscreen.

Night creams tend to be a bit heavier and are more treatment-oriented. As you sleep, your body relaxes, which means that your skin relaxes. It's an ideal time to start working a bit of magic on tired, sagging facial skin. Night creams will help to rejuvenate elasticity and provide you with a revitalized canvas in the morning.

Naturally, as with all product choices and skin care needs, you are the ultimate judge of what your skin needs and what it doesn't. But keep in mind that using the same moisturizer day and night is akin to wearing the same clothes out for dinner that you wore to the office. Sometimes it works, but sometimes you want something that's different.

When it comes to applying a moisturizer, most people think of simply smoothing the cream, lotion, or gel across the face. Truer coverage, however, can be achieved by pouring or scooping the moisturizer into your hands, rubbing your hands together to spread the product, and then applying it to your face and neck in a wide sweeping motion. This gives a more thorough coverage, and more thorough coverage means better-feeling (and better-looking) skin.

You may also decide to use a moisturizer that has been created specifically for the delicate skin around the eyes. After years of smiling, frowning, squinting, and just general living, one of the first areas to show signs of wear and tear is the eye area. Tiny lines and wrinkles form. They used to be called "crow's feet." The more politically correct term these days is "laugh lines." It sounds nicer, but the damage is the same.

Eye creams are not miracle cures, and they don't physically change the structure of skin. They also won't get rid of dark circles or extreme puffiness. But they do help. A little dab around the eye area, concentrating specifically in the areas where lines are visible, will soften the skin around the eyes so that when you laugh, cry, frown, or squint, the lines will be less noticeable and you will look a bit younger than before.

The lips are also prone to dryness and chapping. Try a healing balm of some sort, or use a bit of eye cream after you've cleansed.

SKIN CARE: A SUMMARY

Follow the three-step cleansing, toning, moisturizing skin care plan every morning and night at least. If you work out during the day, your skin care regimen might be morning, noon, and night. Getting yourself into a routine of the skin care basics is an important part in the care and feeding of your skin. You'll look better, you'll feel better, and your skin will thank you for years to come.

In addition, excessive use of tobacco, alcohol, or drugs can contribute to premature aging of the skin. Nicotine in tobacco affects the blood vessels and slows circulation. Alcohol dilates the blood vessels, although light intake of alcoholic beverages, especially wine, may not be harmful to the skin. It's the heavy, regular intake of alcohol that may cause blood vessels to dilate until tiny vessels burst in the white of the eyeball and beneath the skin. Excessive alcohol intake can cause the eyes to become puffy and can contribute to dehydrated, sagging skin.

Skin Types

Knowing your skin type is important because it will tell you what types of products you should use and what you should avoid. It will also help you to take better care of your skin, both externally and internally.

Determining skin type is easy. The first thing you need to determine is how much oil your skin produces. Do this by looking in a mirror. After cleansing your face, take a look at your skin. Be objective. Look for blackheads: these are good indicators of problems and problem areas. Blackheads indicate clogged pores, and this means that your skin is releasing more oil than your pores can handle. You should also note if the blackheads are concentrated in specific areas like the nose, chin, or forehead. This area, commonly known as the *T-zone,* can be treated differently from the rest of your face once you identify your overall skin type.

Now that you have an idea of oil production, ask yourself these questions.

1. Do you have any areas of redness?

2. Do you have broken capillaries, and if so, where?

3. Do you have any sensitivities to specific products?

4. Have you had a lot of sun exposure in the past?

5. Does your skin ever peel?

6. Does it ever feel tight?

The answers to these questions will help you to determine your skin type.

DEHYDRATED SKIN

Contrary to what you may think, dehydrated skin is not lacking in oil. Rather, it is lacking in water. The skin cells aren't retaining water as they should, and this causes the skin cells to build up. This buildup can be removed with exfoliation, but you still need to understand why skin is dehydrated in the first place in order to keep it from happening again.

While some people are genetically predisposed to having dehydrated skin, making it more difficult to treat, others can address the dehydration problem more easily. If you live in a desert climate, you'll have more trouble keeping skin hydrated than someone who lives in a more humid climate. Combat this by getting yourself a humidifier and drinking more water.

Other factors that contribute to dehydrated skin are sun, soap, and flying. Cleanse, moisturize, and rehydrate as quickly as you can after engaging in any of these activities.

DRY SKIN

Dry skin occurs when the sebaceous (oil) glands don't produce enough oil to keep the outer skin moist. The condition can be genetic, like dehydrated skin, but can also be influenced by age and climate. Dry climates can cause a decrease in oil gland production, just as hot climates can cause oil glands to increase production. Keep in mind that getting older does not mean that your skin stops producing oil.

OILY SKIN

As the name of this skin type indicates, oily skin is caused by too much oil production. Oily skin can have any number of problems, like acne, blackheads, and more.

Once again, genetics can play a role in whether or not you have oily skin. Diet and climate are the next biggest culprits. A hot summer day combined with the sweat produced by exercise can wreak havoc on oily skin. Hormonal changes, like those brought on by puberty, are also big contributors to oily skin.

COMBINATION SKIN

Let's talk about the T-zone again for just a minute. The T-zone includes the forehead, nose, and chin. This area is called the T-zone, because the configuration forms a T, and oily skin in only this area will categorize you as having combination skin.

The nose has the highest number of active oil glands; the chin and forehead are next and are about equal in terms of oil production. However, even if you have oily skin in the T-zone, you do not have dry skin on the cheeks. It is impossible to have two such extremes. This type of skin is almost always categorized as "combination," or "normal with an oily T-zone."

NORMAL SKIN

Normal skin functions by producing enough oil not to clog pores but to keep skin properly moist and hydrated. Normal skin doesn't suffer from breakouts nearly as often as other skin types, except perhaps during times of stress, and for that reason, normal skin is rare. If you've got it, enjoy it.

COUPEROSE SKIN

This skin type is characterized by broken capillaries under the surface of the skin. It is often caused by genetics, but most especially by the environment in which you live. Exposure to hot sun, coupled with extreme heat, causes couperose, though it can be hard to see through a tan. Conversely, cold and wind, like the conditions found on ski slopes in the winter, are equally damaging, as are alcohol and smoking. Alcohol opens capillaries while smoking constricts them, putting pressure on fragile capillaries.

This skin type is also something that's unavoidable. All people experience some form of couperose skin as they get older. The only thing you can do is to minimize its appearance.

SENSITIVE SKIN

Sensitive skin can be defined as skin that feels sensitive and skin that is actually sensitive to the touch. Skin that feels sensitive will itch, burn, and feel—though not necessarily look—irritated when certain products are applied. You probably already know if you have sensitive skin because you've been experiencing it for years. You probably also don't know exactly what causes sensitive skin, though one thing that probably does is fragrance in your skin care products.

As with most skin types, sensitive skin is inherited. Other factors, such as chemical peels or laser resurfacing, along with prolonged sun exposure, can also lead to a sensitive skin type. The wind, the cold, the heat, the dog, the cat—they all can irritate and make sensitive skin even worse.

SUN-DAMAGED SKIN

This type of skin cannot be inherited and can be prevented. Skin that has been damaged by the sun is rough to the look and feel; it's dry and usually has a number of deep wrinkles. The outer layer appears thicker and is commonly described as "leathery." Sun-damaged skin also appears perpetually tan, even when it isn't. Unfortunately, because sun-damaged skin is damaged, there isn't a lot that can be done to remedy it except for plastic surgery or a face-lift.

MATURE SKIN

Mature skin is a term applied to people who are older. It is not truly a skin type because it is not categorized as oily or dry, or firm or sagging. The term is arbitrary more than anything else: every skin type has special needs—not just older skin.

Skin Colors

Skin type is also directly related to skin color. Human skin contains four types of pigment: melanin, oxygenated hemoglobin, reduced hemoglobin, and carotenes. Melanin is the dark brown or black pigment that's responsible for hair, skin, and eye color. It's the most potent pigment and is what causes the skin to become darker as it tans. The cells that produce melanin are called *melanocytes* and are considered to be identical in all races. A square inch of skin on an adult contains approximately 60,000 melanocytes. It's known that the depth of melanin in the skin can affect the color of the skin. Its structure and additional effects are still being studied.

Hemoglobin is the pigment that gives red blood cells their color. When hemoglobin is oxygenated (combined with oxygen), it produces a healthy color to the skin. When hemoglobin is lacking oxygen, or is oxygen-reduced, the skin regardless of color, takes on a pale or bluish color.

Carotenes are pigments that give a yellow tone to the skin. A yellow cast can be caused by eating too many foods that are yellow or orange (oranges, carrots, etc). This condition is known as *carotenoderma*. It also causes the whites of the eyes to look yellowish. Although jaundice causes the skin to take on a yellowish cast, it is not caused by carotene. It's a disease of the liver, and the color results from bile pigments in the blood.

When the pigments of the skin are unevenly distributed, the skin will have lighter and darker areas, such as freckles. Darker skin contains more melanin granules and will tan more quickly than light skin. Certain diseases interfere with the production of melanin and can cause the skin to become blotchy. Any change in the normal color of the skin should be brought to the attention of a dermatologist. There are no known permanent ways to change the basic color of skin.

SHAVING

Part of being a man is learning how to groom your beard or lack thereof. Whiskers can be a welcome addition to a sexy look (remember Sean Connery in *The Hunt for Red October*) or a real pain to you and to her. Keeping your face groomed means shaving and trimming.

Because beard grain is similar to hair grain, you should have a working knowledge of how your beard grows. The general rule is that whiskers grow down, except on the lower half of the neck, where they grow up. There are exceptions, of course. Sometimes the neck hair grows down only, with no upward growth, and sometimes the hair grows toward the side of the neck. If you shave with a safety razor or an old-fashioned straight-edge razor, you probably know exactly how your beard grows and you shave accordingly.

Home shaving is something all men do at one time or another. Some men have a relatively light beard; others have a "shadow" within several hours of shaving. Some men shave with soap, others with shaving cream. Some use a razor, others use an electric device. Whatever method you prefer, the art of shaving is just that: an art.

SHAVING AS ART

Several decades ago, shaving was one of the services most frequently performed in a barber shop. Today, however, most men shave at home, causing the art of shaving to be almost lost. Why? It's generally considered quicker and easier to shave yourself at home, incorporating shaving into your everyday routine.

There are still barber shops, however, where shaves are available for those who wish them. Usually these are either full-service, luxury salons or the more traditional, established shops where the service has been offered for many years. One thing remains constant: The art of shaving requires a great deal of attention, skill, and practice.

FUNDAMENTALS OF SHAVING

The objective of shaving is to remove the visible part of facial and neck hair without irritating the skin. The professional barber-stylist uses a straight razor and warm lather when shaving a client.

Although there are certain general principles of shaving that apply to all men, there are also certain exceptions that need to be considered. The texture of the hair, the grain of the beard, and the sensitivity of the skin to the razor edge, shaving cream, hot towels, or astringent lotion all factor into the decision about how to proceed with the shave.

Hot towels should not be used when the skin is chapped or blistered from heat or cold, or when the skin is thin and sensitive. Astringents may also be too harsh for this type of skin.

Curly facial hair has its own inherent characteristics that may cause problems if the shave isn't performed correctly. All too often, ingrown hairs are the result of improper hair removal by a razor, tweezer, or trimmer. Curly hair has the tendency to grow in a "looped" direction and as it grows out of the skin, it can bend back into the skin surface. Excessively close shaving, coupled with excessive pressure, with either clippers, trimmers, or razors can damage skin to the point that new hair growth is trapped under the injured tissue. This can result in infected bumps on and under the skin surface, scar tissue, or a keloid condition.

THE TOOLS OF THE TRADE

Razors are the sharpest and most delicate cutting instruments available. They can be used for facial shaves, neck shaves, finish work, and even in haircutting.

Conventional Straight Razors

The straight razor is comprised of a hardened steel blade attached to a handle by means of a pivot. The handle is made of either hard rubber, plastic, or bone.

The following factors should be considered when choosing a straight razor: balance, temper, grind, finish, size and style.

1. *Razor balance*—This is the weight and length of the blade relative to the handle. In a properly balanced straight razor, the weight of the blade and the handle are equal. Balance is important for safety. If a razor is not well balanced, the head will move up or down.

2. *Razor temper*—This does not mean that an angry razor will hurt you. It simply refers to the special heat treatment given by the manufacturer. When a razor is properly tempered, it acquires a degree of hardness required for good cutting or shaving. Hard-tempered razors will hold an edge longer, but are hard to sharpen. Soft-tempered razors are easy to sharpen, but don't hold an edge very long.

3. *Razor grinds*—This is the shape of the razor, either concave or wedge, after it's been ground. Concave grinds are generally preferred because the back and the edge look hollow. Beard resistance can be more easily felt with a concave razor. A wedge grind is one where both sides of the blade form a sharp angle at the extreme edge of the razor. For obvious reasons, this is a more difficult blade to master and can be perceived as more dangerous. It is, however, a wonderful razor for coarse, heavy beards.

4. *Razor finish*—This is the material on the surface, often plain steel, polished steel, or metal-plated. Of all of these, the polished steel finish is the most expensive, but it also lasts longer. The metal-plated razors often experience a worn-off finish that has tried to conceal a poor-quality steel.

HONES

Hones are used to sharpen razors. Many types are available, giving different types of edges for different types of shaves. When it comes to choosing a hone, personal preference wins out. Here are some varieties.

1. *Natural hones*—Derived from rock deposits, these hones are used wet. A water hone, imported from Germany, is a slow-cutting hone that produces a lasting edge. The Belgian hone is also a slow-cutting hone, but a little faster than the water hone with a very sharp edge.

2. *Synthetic hones*—These are manufactured hones called the Swaty hone and the carborundum hone. Because they cut faster than water hones, these synthetic hones have the advantage of producing a keen cutting edge in less time.

3. *Combination hones*—As you might guess, these hones are both water and synthetic, giving you the choice of either the synthetic edge when the razor is bad or the water side when the razor needs a slight touch-up.

Honing is the process of sharpening the razor with smooth, even strokes of equal number and pressure on both sides of the blade.

NOT SHAVING

If you decide to grow a moustache or beard, you might need a few general grooming tips. After all, both have been worn by men of every social class throughout history, and have often been used to signify social status.

The moustache is worn primarily for personal adornment rather than utility. Chances are, if you're a moustache wearer, you're fairly particular about how it looks. Knowing how to trim and shape a moustache is very important.

Facial structure, hair growth, and personal taste must all be considered. The size of your moustache should correspond with and complement the size of your facial features.

- large, coarse facial features—heavy moustache
- prominent nose—medium to large moustache

- long, narrow face—narrow to medium moustache
- extra-large mouth—pyramid-shaped moustache
- extra-small mouth—medium, short moustache
- smallish, regular features—small, triangular moustache
- wide mouth with prominent upper lip—heavy handlebar or large, divided moustache
- round face with regular features—semi-square moustache
- square face with prominent features—heavy, linear moustache with ends curving slightly downward

In designing and trimming your moustache, always consider these important factors: length of mouth, size of nose, upper lip area, width of cheeks, jaw and chin, and density of hair growth.

Moustache Trimming

Thin the moustache with a comb and shears. Trim the moustache to the desired length with shears. Check the length for evenness at the corner of the mouth. Shape the moustache with a razor or trimmer. You can also wax the ends, pencil in temporary color with crayons (see Chapter 7), or even color your moustache for overall color evenness.

Beard Design and Trimming

Beards are great for balancing facial features and correlating proportions of face, head, and body. Beard trimming usually is performed with shears, comb, clippers, and razor.

Trim excess hair with shears and comb. Draw the desired beard design with an eyebrow pencil. Starting in the middle, directly under the chin, outline the under part of the beard, working to the right side of the face up to the sideburn and ear area. Repeat for the left side. Taper and blend the beard from the outlined areas up to just under the bottom lip, moustache, and cheek areas. Outline the cheek and upper areas of the beard, blending with the sideburn area. If you're using a razor, massage shaving lather into the area of the beard to be shaved. Shave the unwanted part of the beard. Remove the lather and penciled beard design. You might want to use an after-shave lotion.

Trim and blend the moustache. Check and retouch the beard with shears and comb wherever necessary. Recomb or restyle the hair as needed for a finished look.

You can also use a clipper for trimming your beard, especially if one overall length is desired. Clipper cut beard trims are most successful if your beard has an even density and texture.

One last thing where beards are concerned: Remember to blend hair color as well as hair length into your beard.

SHAVING YOUR HEAD

Some men, whether losing their hair or not, choose to go absolutely bald and shave their heads. This is a process that is difficult to do alone because it requires applying a sharp instrument to your scalp. It's best to have this done professionally or with the help of someone you trust with your life.

If you do choose to have your head shaved at home, start with a clipper-razor and cut the hair as close to the scalp as possible. Then lather up your head using your preferred shaving cream or soap, and hand the straight razor to your partner. The shaving should go against the grain of the hair, similar to how whiskers are shaved, in order to get the closest shave possible. Proceed slowly and carefully.

When finished, wipe away the excess lather, run your hands over your scalp to feel for excess hairs, and then apply a lotion of your choice.

KEEPING UP WITH YOUR CUT

Keeping up with your cut is a lot easier than you think. But you must pay attention to what your hair needs.

The Dos

- Do shampoo on a daily basis to keep your hair healthy and happy. When you keep the hair and scalp clean, you keep dandruff at bay, add a healthy shine, and keep your hair in shape.

- Do use your hands as a comb. Running your hands through your hair to put it back into place puts much less wear and tear on your hair, and makes your life a whole lot easier. It's also quite freeing; it means you can't have every hair in place. The result is a carefree, casual look. Besides, when you use your hands, you've always got a comb right at your fingertips.

- Do massage your scalp.

- Do get a haircut every six to eight weeks.

- Do have fun with your hair. It's okay to experiment with different styling tools and application techniques. It's even okay to occasionally change your hair cut. Change is good, even for your hair.

As trends come and go and fashion dictates our style, always remember that hair, hopefully, is here to stay. It's proper care and feeding is in your hands, and like any other organism, it depends on you for a long, healthy, and happy life. Take its care seriously.

Cheers.

Index